Day by Day

through the NEW TESTAMENT

ACTS to
REVELATION

Also by C. Wiliam Nichols
published by Chalice Press

Storytelling the Gospel

Day by Day through the New Testament: The Gospels

Day by Day

through the NEW TESTAMENT

ACTS to
REVELATION

C. William Nichols

CHALICE
PRESS
ST. LOUIS, MISSOURI

Cover photo: © Digital Stock
Cover and interior design: Elizabeth Wright
Art direction: Elizabeth Wright

This book is printed on acid-free, recycled paper.

Visit Chalice Press on the World Wide Web at
www.chalicepress.com

10 9 8 7 6 5 4 3 2 1   02 03 04 05 06

Library of Congress Cataloging–in–Publication Data

Nichols, C. William.
    Day by day through the New Testament : Acts–Revelation / by C. William Nichols.
        p.   cm.
    ISBN 0-8272-0629-1
    1. Bible. N.T. Acts–Meditations.   2. Bible. N.T. Epistles–Meditations.
3. Bible. N.T. Revelation–Meditations. 4. Devotional calendars.   I. Title.
    BS2617.8 .N53 2002
    242'.5–dc21   2001006458

Printed in the United States of America

Dedicated, in loving memory,
to these saints in heaven:
Claude and Beulah Nichols
and
Claud and Margaret Shewmake.
"They rest from their labors."

INTRODUCTION

Dear Reader:

I have been most gratified by the response to my first book in this series, *Day by Day through the New Testament: The Gospels.* That work was undertaken in acknowledgment of what I perceive to be a widespread hunger for a greater understanding of the Bible, and a frustration that a simple, day-by-day reading plan was not available.

From childhood I have had a great love for the Bible and have committed many of its more familiar passages to memory. Those favorite texts have frequently come to my consciousness in times of need and have been doorways through which I have come into the presence of the living God.

Through the years I have developed a favorite method of reading scripture. I read a portion of it (a chapter or less), slowly and with my full attention to the reading. Then I ask God to lift out of the reading some portion that says something God wants me to know, and that I need to know, that day. Often what happens is what I like to call a "tangent of the Holy Spirit." It may not be a thought I have had before, and it may not be the primarily intended message of the scriptural reading. But it is the product of the living, creative presence of God, and the often-confusing mixture of needs and understandings I bring to the scripture, and the wonderfully inventive Holy Spirit. Then I close my contemplation with a short prayer that is suggested by the scripture and my experience at the moment.

This book, as well as the first one in the series, is arranged to accommodate to that reading plan. First, a scripture reading is indicated. Please read the scripture first, before reading my reflection on it. It will enrich your experience so much more if you will read that scripture every day. In fact, I strongly suggest that you keep your Bible with this book, so that you will not be tempted to omit the scripture reading for the day.

Then, once you have read both the indicated scripture and the reflection, take a few moments to express your own thoughts Godward. I did not conclude each day's reflection with a printed sentence or two of prayer, because I believe that what I might say in a prayer would probably not coincide with what you will want and need to say to God as a result of your reading of the scripture and the reflection. But like the scripture, this too is a most important part of the complete devotional experience.

Can you spare five or six minutes a day to deepen your spiritual life and equip yourself for your discipleship? Following the procedure I outlined above will accomplish that in no more time than the few minutes suggested.

And once you have finished the first book (on the gospels) and this second book on the rest of the New Testament, you will have read through the complete New Testament, in consecutive and comprehensive daily passages.

As a personal note, through the two years that these two books have been in preparation, I read through the complete New Testament, leaving not one word out, beginning with Matthew 1:1, and ending with Revelation 22:21, and I must say that it was a life-changing experience. I'm glad I did it, and I believe you will share that joy when you do the same.

God love you, every one,
C. William Nichols

DAY 1
Read Acts 1

In their final meeting with Jesus, the disciples showed how much they needed the experience of a time of prayer and preparation before they were ready to represent the Christ to a world that did not know him. With a new ethic of love and a new promise of wholeness to proclaim to a needy world, their only question was a political one: "Lord, is this time when you will restore the kingdom to Israel?" It was almost in exasperation that Jesus replied, "It is not for you to know the times or periods that the Father has set by his own authority."

It was as if Jesus were saying to his followers, "That is not your business. That is God's business. God will handle it." But then Jesus told them what their business was: "But you will receive power when the Holy Spirit has come upon you; and you will be my witnesses." There was a magnificent obsession that would consume the rest of their lives–to go into all the world and proclaim the gospel of Christ. But before they were ready to begin that historic endeavor, they must first receive from God the power by which they would be capable of doing it.

In our pragmatic and activist age, being a Christian is frequently seen as a matter of doing the right thing and making the most helpful contributions to a world that limps along in its discovery of the divine purpose. And certainly all our best efforts are needed and justified. But Christianity is not so much something that we do, as something that we are, and only then what we do as a result of what we are.

A teacher in a missionary school for boys in India was well known for his patience, even in the most trying circumstances. He was often asked where he got his patience. He always replied, somewhat cryptically, "It grows in my garden." One day a group of his students showed up at his house and demanded to see that famous garden where such amazing patience grew. The teacher led them through his house, out the back door, and into a narrow, cheerless enclosure. When the students expressed disappointment in its lack of beauty and character, the teacher replied, "No, it is not very long, and not very wide. But," he added as he lifted his eyes heavenward, "it is very, very tall."

Don't neglect that garden where your faith grows.

The strange and exciting events of Pentecost had roots that ran back, through misty memory, to an ancient time, a common problem, and a helpful suggestion from an unlikely source. The place was the wilderness of Sinai in the odyssey of the people of Israel from Egypt's bondage to their promised land. Moses, though still a wise and vigorous leader in his eighth decade of life, was finding it difficult to settle all the petty disputes of the contentious people he undertook to lead. Seeing his frustration and weariness, Jethro—Moses' father-in-law—urged Moses to appoint good and wise leaders who would share the burden of responsibility. So Moses, after consulting God in prayer, appointed seventy "elders," who would constitute the board of leadership (later to be known as the Sanhedrin.) Each of the seventy was given a special portion of God's grace to equip him for his leadership role.

But while these seventy fulfilled their divinely appointed role and spoke on God's behalf as prophets, there were two other men of faith—Eldad and Medad—who also spoke on God's behalf and taught the people. Naturally, the regularly appointed elders were offended by the unauthorized actions of these imposters, and appealed to Moses to command them to cease their prophesying. They were not members of the union! They did not carry the proper credentials!

But Moses demonstrated magnanimity and perhaps a glimpse into God's ultimate plan when he answered their complaints, "Would that all the LORD's people were prophets, and that the LORD would put his spirit on them!" (Numbers 11:29). How wonderful it would be if every person were a priest, a prophet endowed by the Holy Spirit! Such was Moses' dream.

Centuries later, the prophet Joel picked up the refrain of Moses' dream, and foretold the day when it would become a reality. "Then afterward," Joel said, "I will pour out my spirit on all flesh; your sons and your daughters shall prophesy, your old men shall dream dreams, and your young men shall see visions" (Joel 2:28).

And at last on the day of Pentecost, the dream of Moses and the vision of Joel became fact! It is the plan and the intention of God that every person should be given the gift of holy endowment and the challenge of divine purpose.

Whatever else may have been accomplished in that historic and eventful day of the church's birth, it also issued you the license that gives you the power and the promise of the Holy God, to act on God's behalf in this world. Claim your inheritance!

DAY 3
Read Acts 3

It was a most dramatic and instructive event: the healing of the lame man at the gate of the temple in Jerusalem. It was the first time a miracle of healing was attributed to followers of Jesus. But note that Peter and John were quick to point out that the credit for the healing did not belong to them, but to the one in whose name the miracle was performed. They said to the curious crowd that gathered around the scene of the healing, "You Israelites, why do you wonder at this, or why do you stare at us, as though by our own power or piety we had made him walk?" "In the name of Jesus Christ of Nazareth," they had said, as the healing took place.

It was an important principle, and one that had to be restated again and again, as the followers of Jesus accomplished works that appeared to be quite beyond the reach of human strength or piety. It was not their power, but Christ's; it was not their righteousness, but the Lord's. They were simply instruments in the transmitting of divine grace to answer human need.

But rather than diminishing their role in this process, Peter and John acknowledged one of the most glorious privileges of our discipleship: that God is willing to condescend to us, to give us access to powers not deserved by our own faith or character. But note this: such powers are given to us only when we are representing God in providing for someone else's needs.

One of the great foundation stones of the Christian movement—and one that was restated in the Protestant Reformation—is the priesthood of every believer. Those tongues of fire—representing the endowment of the Holy Spirit—rested on the heads of all who were present. We do not know how many people were present, or what their experience with Christ had been. But it is clear that such a manifestation was not limited to the apostles. And in that great text from Joel, upon which Peter based his sermon, God had said, "I will pour out my spirit upon all flesh"—all people!

Imagine the honor, the absolute glory, of being a link between divine grace and human need. And that audacious glory is ours when we let ourselves be used as tools in God's hand—"instruments," as St. Francis put it in his memorable prayer, "of thy peace."

And it is that glorious privilege that Pentecost reveals to you.

Very early in its history, the church began to experience the persecutions of an establishment that felt threatened by the new spirit demonstrated so magnificently in the lives and actions of the early Christians. The new is always subjected to the paranoia of the old. And the spectacular event of the healing of a lame man at the gate of the temple was the spark that detonated the resentment of the Jewish authorities that had been growing ever since Jesus had first publicly questioned their monopolistic claim on the truth.

The authorities seemed to have all the ammunition on their side. Peter and John—and most of the other Christians—were common people, with little education or theological sophistication. Their experience in religious matters was scarcely three years long. They could not have hoped to win any debates with their adversaries. They had no precedents to offer, no history of ecclesiastical connection. But they had two assets, which assured them of victory against their accusers.

First, they had the evidence of a man who had clearly been healed. When the establishmentarians, in their robes of office, approached Peter and John in the temple, they saw, standing with them, the man who had been healed. And when they saw him standing, on two good and strong legs, in their midst, they had nothing to say in opposition. Results always speak more loudly than any words. The early Christians won their case, time and time again, not by brilliant argument, but by unquestionable results.

The way of Christ works. It did then, and it does now. There is a host of empirical evidence to support that claim, and most of us would have to look no further than our own lives to discover it.

But the disciples had another asset that gave them confidence, and the Jewish authorities recognized it. When they saw the boldness of Peter and John, they recognized that they had been with Jesus. That's the point! They had spent hours in the presence of the Christ, and something in that association had given them qualities of character and a strength of purpose that were beyond the reach of human achievement.

Can your family and friends tell, from your manner, your speech, your actions, that you have spent time with your Lord?

As vigorously as science condemns superstition, one must concede that behind some of the cautionary superstitions there may be a grain of truth. Walking under a ladder might, indeed, presage "bad luck," unless you consider the possibility of getting a bucket of paint dropped on your head "good luck." And breaking a mirror does, indeed, result in the misfortune of having to go out and purchase a new one.

So, before we ridicule those who, according to the scriptural record, crowded around Peter in the hope that the shadow of this good man might fall upon them, let us consider what grain of truth might have impelled them to do such a thing. To get within the range of the shadow of Peter meant, obviously, that they had to bring themselves close to him. And being close to Peter would surely result in being influenced by his faith and sharing in the radiance of his transformed personality. There was no magic here, only the natural consequence of companionship with someone of great spiritual stature.

There is no report of any beneficial result of this closeness to Peter, but one must conclude that those upon whom the shadow of Peter fell would derive some blessing from that closeness.

There are two ways to look at this phenomenon. First, we must recognize that there is a magnificent effect stemming from our closeness to people of piety and power. We tend to assume a likeness to those whom we admire enough to seek their presence. When we spend time in the presence of intelligent people, we begin to share in their perceptions. When we are in company with those who are pure in heart, our lives begin to take on their virtues.

But we are also reminded, by the tiny detail in this scripture, of the unconscious influence our presence will have upon those who are close enough to us that our shadow falls on them. Think of those who will be near enough to you today that your shadow falls on them: members of your family, your coworkers, your neighbors, those who may be looking to you for some help. Will your shadow bless them?

It was inevitable, but disappointing all the same: Early in its life the church suffered a division in its ranks. "They were all together in one accord," the record states of the first Christians on the day of Pentecost, when the church was born. But as the ranks of the church multiplied, differences of perception and opinion sundered the once-unified church.

The cause of the rift resulted from the church's acts of benevolence. Food was distributed to the widows and others incapable of providing for themselves. But, as the saying goes, "No good deed goes unpunished." And the punishment for this compassionate response to the needs of the destitute was the suspicion that the munificence was not distributed equitably. The Christians of Greek descent complained that the widows of their ethnic group were not dealt with as generously as were those of Hebrew ancestry. One might have hoped that once they became Christians, that new identity would have lifted them above ethnic divisions. That was the principle Paul articulated in his Galatian letter: "There is no longer Jew or Greek, there is no longer slave or free, there is no longer male and female; for you all of you are one in Christ Jesus" (Galatians 3:28).

But that principle was still a dream, and the early Christians allowed their political partisanship to divide them. It was a regrettable evidence of their as-yet-incomplete understanding of the essential unbrokenness of the body of Christ.

The apostles dealt with that schism in a most helpful way, in the appointing of deacons to oversee the daily distributions and assure the even-handed treatment of all those in need.

But the church is still plagued by divisions that result from lesser allegiances. We have yet to discover the unity of the church and the realization that all God's children constitute one family.

Whether the impecunious widows (and others in need) are Greek or Jewish is of no consequence. What is important for Christians to remember is that they are our brothers and sisters in Christ.

DAY 7
Read Acts 7

Nobody told Stephen, when he allowed his name to be on the ballot in the first election of deacons, that he would be expected to be a Bible scholar! After all, he did not grow up in the faith. His Greek name suggests that he was one of the Gentiles who were added to the church in the earliest days of its history. Surely there would be time, in the three years or so of his tenure of office, to take a few Bible classes.

But he could still feel that holy impress of ordaining hands on his head when he was called on to defend not only his faith, but also his life. And his defense had to be made while standing before the world's foremost authorities on Hebrew law and history.

So what did Stephen do? Did he say, "Well, I'm only a layman…" or "If I had known I was going to have to take a test, I would have studied a little"? No, somewhat to our surprise—and to the unquestionable consternation of the Sanhedrin—Stephen rose to the occasion with remarkable poise and wisdom. He traced the history of the Hebrew people with clarity and insight, finding parallels there that defended his own beliefs.

It is interesting that the Sanhedrin offered no counterarguments. It was as though Stephen's expertise in the subject left them muttering in their beards, with no recourse but to kill him.

In a classic "Peanuts" comic strip, Lucy is chasing Charlie Brown, shouting, "I'll get you, Charlie Brown. I'll catch you, and when I do, I'm going to knock your block off!" Suddenly Charlie Brown screeches to a halt. He turns around and says, "Wait a minute, Lucy. If you and I, as relatively small children with relatively small problems, can't sit down and talk through our problems in a mature way, how can we expect the nations of the world to…" Then POW! Lucy slugs him. She says, "I had to hit him quick. He was beginning to make sense."

And that is precisely what the Sanhedrin did to poor Stephen. They had to hit him quick, because he was beginning to make sense. It was beginning to show clearly, in Stephen's recitation of Hebrew history, that God's enemies were always those who refused to accept new truth when it was given to them. The staunch defenders of the status quo will wake up, one day, to discover that God's parade has passed them by.

There was an official list of the kinds of people who would not be admitted to the Hebrew faith. Deuteronomy 23:1 specifically lists eunuchs as members of this group. No matter whether they had been castrated by accident, or as an injury in war, or in an act of self-mutilation, eunuchs were forever barred from "the assembly of the LORD." Numbered with the eunuchs were illegitimate children and their descendants, Amorites and Moabites, and various other groups of people. They were the *index expurgatorious* of the Jews. No matter what they did or did not do, they were forever barred from the company of the righteous.

What a breath of fresh air it must have been to the many who had thus been excluded, to find in the Christian community a ready welcome for all people.

That is precisely the point of the story of the Ethiopian eunuch, to whom the deacon Philip witnessed, and whom he baptized. Here was a eunuch, and a foreigner. He could never have gained admittance to the communion of the Hebrew faithful, but he was worth a long trek, by foot, by one of the officers of the new church.

But though it is not specifically stated in the report of this incident, one may safely conclude that there were those in the Christian community who resented the introduction into their society of one so totally lacking in the character and background of the members of their establishment. How could they share their Christian faith with one of his race? Surely one must draw the line somewhere! And the line they would have drawn would definitely have left the Ethiopian eunuch on the outside!

It is both ironic and tragic that many Christian people are so obsessed with deciding which people may–and which may not–be recipients of the grace of God. If weighing the credentials of anyone who wants to be a part of Christ's church is a worthy activity, let us first consider our own poverty of qualifications. If God's grace can reach as far as our own needs and frailties, who can doubt that God can reach far enough to include anyone, however unqualified they may seem to us.

Christ welcomes many to his fellowship who would never be admitted to many country clubs, or fraternal organizations, or civic clubs, or social sororities. The sole criteria upon which the church must base its membership policies are these: the need of God's grace, and the willingness to accept it through the mediation of Jesus Christ.

DAY 9
Read Acts 9

We all know the power of a "word fitly spoken." Think of those occasions when a word of encouragement, coming at the right time, gave you the courage to try again—and to succeed. Do you remember occasions when someone's simple word of friendship or concern pierced the gloom of depression with the sunrise of joy? And no one can measure the transforming power of a sincere word of forgiveness that knits a raveled relationship.

Words fitly spoken have sometimes been the pivots upon which historic events have turned. Who can measure the staggering cost of Hitler's words in his *Mein Kampf,* or the power of Churchill's call to courage, "We shall never give up, never give up, never give up"?

But never was a word more fitly spoken than that day a blind, chastened, and confused Saul of Tarsus, following the puzzling instruction of the risen Christ, met a Damascus Christian to obtain further instructions in the process of his conversion.

Ananias had also received a visit from the resurrected Christ. He was told that Saul was waiting for him at a certain house. As far as Ananias knew, Saul was still the church's "public enemy number one." But Christ told him, "He is a chosen instrument of mine." It wasn't much, but it was a divine word, and Ananias was an obedient Christian. So, when Ananias came to the house where Saul was staying, in that historic moment, the Christian laid his hands on the persecutor and said, "Brother..."

Can there be any doubt that the one word "brother"—however much it might have cost Ananias to say it—did more to bring Saul into the Christian faith than any other word could have done? What a powerful word! What a healing word! What a welcoming word! It was a word that opened the door to the enormous contribution Paul the apostle would make to the church, and to the world.

The words you speak have power to bless, or, when those words are left unspoken, to curse. Most of us speak several thousand words a day. Perhaps they are of no consequence. Would you care to tell that to Christ? He reminded us, "By your words you will be justified, and by your words you will be condemned" (Matthew 12:37). Have your words, today, forgiven anyone, encouraged anyone, or invited anyone into Christ's kingdom of love? Have you called anyone "brother"?

"Can anyone forbid water for baptizing these people?" That was Peter's inquiry when the Roman Cornelius and his family responded, in faith, to the teaching of Christ. The question was not a mere rhetorical question, however, for there were many Christians, at that time, who would have withheld baptism from a family like that of Cornelius.

While there had been people of Greek and Roman descent who had become Christians (notably all seven of the newly elected deacons in Jerusalem), each of them had come to Christ through the Jewish tradition. They had been circumcised in order to conform to the law of Moses. But Cornelius had not become a Jew, and apparently felt no need to do so. He was a military officer stationed in Caesaria, which was the seat of the Roman government in Palestine. But he was also a God-fearing man and a compassionate one. He was one of a large—and growing—number of Romans who could no longer stomach the traditional paganism of Rome and, longing for a God they could believe in, had turned to the Jewish faith. They had not accepted all the rules and rituals of Judaism, but they believed in one God and were motivated by that belief to live morally and ethically upright lives. But Cornelius was ready for something more.

Then one day, at three o'clock in the afternoon, Cornelius was praying to God, and God answered his prayer, telling the astonished Roman officer where he could find help in the spiritual growth he needed to make.

There is much to commend in Cornelius, and he can be seen as an exemplar of a new direction for the church of Jesus Christ, which had previously not welcomed Gentiles into the faith. But think just of this fact: Cornelius, though he was a believer in God, and lived an exemplary life, knew that something was still missing in his religious experience, and that need and his closeness to God in prayer opened his heart to seek the resource he needed for taking the next step, which would bring him to Christ.

Even the apostle Paul, toward the end of his spectacular ministry as the church's greatest leader after Christ, confessed that he did not feel that he had accomplished perfection, but even at that advanced age, he trudged on in that path of new inspiration and deeper commitment.

No matter where you are in your Christian discipleship, remember that Christ's call is always a "Heavenly Call" (Philippians 3:14).

If the Jewish authorities martyred Stephen as a deterrent to the new religious movement of the Christians, they must have been mystified to find that their violence against the church had exactly the opposite effect! The Christians were galvanized, energized, and organized by Stephen's death. There was no question, now, that their faith demanded their complete consecration. The church simply could not afford "summer soldiers and sunshine patriots." The persecution and martyrdom of many of the early followers provided the terrible fuel that fired the passion of the church.

The positive spirit of the early Christians was able to take even the most devastating occurrence and turn it to an advantage. When the Christians were forced by persecution to leave Jerusalem, they simply founded another "holy city" in Antioch, where the church prospered and grew.

During the Second World War, the courageous Norwegians had an underground resistance movement against the Nazi regime. Their heroism was kept at a high level by the encouragement of a hymn they frequently sang:

That cause can neither be lost nor stayed
Which takes the course of what God has made,
And is not trusting in walls or towers,
But slowly growing from seeds to flowers.
Be then no more by a storm dismayed,
For by it the full-grown seeds are laid,
And though the tree by its might it shatters,
What then, if thousands of seeds it scatters?

The church knew how to deal with persecution, for it was "born and bred in the briar patch." It began with the death of its founder, and turned that tragedy into the foundation stone of the church's life. And through the intervening centuries, in every age there have been repression and persecution leveled against the church, but the church has not only survived but thrived on its hardships and pains.

And this is a triumphant secret that any Christian can appropriate for his or her own life. As Paul was later to say, "We know that all things work together for good for those who love God, who are called according to his purpose" (Romans 8:28). While we cannot really enjoy our sufferings, we can at least discover what good fruit God hangs on the bitter branches of adversity.

DAY 12
Read Acts 12

King Herod was ostensibly the king of the Jews, but he had obtained that position as a political favor bestowed by the Romans. This Herod had grown up as a pampered courtier in Rome, and though his ancestry could be traced back to the Jewish Herod the Great, this latter-day namesake of the first Herod had done everything to shed his Hebraic image. So when he returned to Israel to occupy the puppet position of king, his first job was to find some way to curry the favor of those over whom he was supposed to rule.

So Herod arrested and martyred James, the first of the apostles to die for their faith. Seeing that this violence against the Christians pleased his Jewish constituents, Herod played his trump card: He had Peter—the titular head of the church—arrested and thrown into jail. Knowing how some Christian leaders in the past had foiled the plans of the authorities to keep them in prison, Herod made special arrangements to keep his notorious prisoner incarcerated. Peter was chained to a guard on either side of him. To assure additional security, special sentries guarded the prison doors. It was almost as secure as that prison-tomb that had contained the dead body of Peter's Lord before Easter.

But in the night, Peter was awakened by an angel who told him, "Get up quickly." And the chains fell off his hands, the guards were put to sleep, the prison doors were opened, and the sentries were asleep at their post. What a string of miraculous helps made Peter's escape from prison possible. But there is one strange detail: Peter was told by the angel, "Dress yourself and put on your sandals." Time was of the essence here. The soldiers might awaken at any moment; the sentries might recover their alertness in time to keep those prison doors locked. And surely the angel who was able to strike the chains off Peter's wrists and open prison doors and put guards and sentries to sleep could have managed that small detail of dressing Peter and putting on his sandals. But God never does for us what we are perfectly capable of doing for ourselves. In the final analysis, then, Peter's miraculous escape from prison depended upon his willingness to do for himself what God would not do for him. What a tragedy it would have been if God had wasted all that divine effort, only to have it all foiled by Peter's unwillingness to do the simple things he could do.

When you ask God today to do for you what you can't, are you sure you have done what you can? God may be waiting to see your contribution as evidence of your faith.

DAY 13
Read Acts 13

It is a great misfortune that the name of Barnabas is rarely recalled when heroes of the faith are listed. Barnabas was quite possibly the most likeable person among all those listed as leaders of the early church. And his contributions to the church were many and indispensable. His undeserved obscurity is due, probably, to the fact that Paul, whose activities on behalf of Christ and the church were similar to those of Barnabas, had his own publicist–Luke. Luke traveled with Paul and carefully recorded the events and teachings of Paul's ministry. If Luke had traveled with Barnabas, surely a similar history could have been written about this dim figure.

The name Barnabas has been translated "son of encouragement." And whether that name was given him at his birth, and he endeavored to live up to it, or whether the name was awarded him because it described his character and personality, surely there can be no doubt that Barnabas was the very embodiment of encouragement. It was his championship of Paul that brought that apostle-to-be back to Antioch from several years of isolation in his home country, to the center of the church's life, where Paul could be trained and set apart for ministry.

It was Barnabas who was willing to forgive Mark for his defection from the leadership team of the first missionary journey, and to invite Mark to join him on another missionary journey.

Barnabas was always there, steady, dependable, performing valuable ministries that never found their way into the headlines. He apparently looked for the best, not the worst, in people. He was always willing to give others a second chance.

And Barnabas did not always have to be "number one." He could follow as well as lead, and as long as Christ was glorified and the church was uplifted, he did not seem to care who received the credit.

What a wonderful joy it is to have a Barnabas in our experience! And the one way to assure that blessing is to be that Barnabas yourself.

DAY 14
Read Acts 14

Lystra was a city in what is present-day Turkey. Though it was under Roman rule during New Testament times, it was Greek in culture and tradition. There was a legend in Lystra that at one time the Greek deities Zeus and Hermes came to the city in human form, searching for hospitality. But no one would receive them except two elderly peasants, Philemon and his wife, Baucis. On the basis of their experience in the city, the Greek gods destroyed all the inhabitants of Lystra except for these two old peasants, who were given the honor of being attendants at the beautiful temple in the city. And when they died they were transformed into great trees that were to live forever.

Without doubt the residents of Lystra knew that legend well, and were conditioned by it to consider the possibility that any stranger in their midst might be a god. So when Paul and Barnabas visited their town and performed an amazing act of healing, the people suspected that they were deities, and began to give them the respect and adulation that would be deserved by gods. Of course, Paul and Barnabas quickly corrected the erroneous assumption of the people and assured them that they were just human beings, as the people were.

Nevertheless, the legend in Lystra and the attitude it fostered in the people suggest a mindset that should be encouraged. It is, in point of fact, the attitude Jesus himself demands of us: we should regard every person we meet as though that person were the very Son of God. And we ought to be as kind, and as compassionate, and as helpful to every person, as we would be to the Christ, if he were suddenly to be in our midst.

In Jesus' parable of the last judgment, the king says to those who are about to receive their eternal reward: "I was hungry and you gave me food, I was thirsty and you gave me something to drink, I was a stranger and you welcomed me, I was naked and you gave me clothing, I was sick and you took care of me, I was in prison and you visited me." But those who are to receive the reward fail to remember any time when they rendered such services to the Lord of Life. But the king says, "As you did it to one of the least of these...you did it to me" (Matthew 25:35–40).

The writer of Hebrews was surely remembering the old story of Abraham when he wrote, "Do not neglect to show hospitality to strangers, for by doing that some have entertained angels without knowing it" (Hebrews 13:2).

That person whom you will meet today on the path of life, who needs your help or encouragement or sympathy or support, will probably not be the Christ in disguise. But can you be sure?

Many years ago, when the stern theology of Calvin governed the church in Scotland, a boy asked his dour pastor if it was permissible for him to ice skate on the Sabbath, provided he skated only to and from church. The grim minister answered, "Well, laddie, it all depends: Will ye or will ye not enjoy the skatin'?"

There was a time when religion and solemnity were regarded as allies, if not twins. If something was enjoyable, that was, in itself, proof of its essential sinfulness. And the converse was also true: If something was religious, it had to be difficult, demanding and joyless. But not everything that tastes bad is good medicine.

Conforming to the Law (which really meant hundreds of laws and requirements) had a certain advantage: it gave people who believed they were faithful in their obedience to the Law the comfortable feeling that they had earned God's love and blessing. How could God not share the kingdom with them, since they had proved their faithfulness? They gained salvation the old-fashioned way: They earned it.

But there were disadvantages to the religion of law. First, very few people were disciplined enough to do all that the law demanded, with the result that for most people the law was more a condemnation than a blessing. But there was an even more serious flaw with the religion of law: it reduced God to an equation and made God's favor a quid pro quo. That is the ultimate blasphemy—believing that we can make ourselves an equal partner with the Eternal One—making ourselves acceptable to God by our acts.

But the Christian faith introduced to the world the concept of grace: the unearned and unmerited favor of God. No, the Gentiles were not worthy of God's love and mercy. But, for that matter, neither were the Jews. Obedience to ten laws will not make us worthy of God's salvation, but neither will our obedience to ten thousand laws. God's favor is not on the sale counter. But God freely gives it to us anyway, because of the merit and mediation of Jesus Christ.

Little wonder the first-century Jews had a difficult time wrapping their minds around the concept of grace, for it passes our understanding, as well. It seems too good to be true.

But in a world designed by God's love, grace is something too good not to be true. And that is the chief source of our joy.

Our life stories are full of forks in the road, and we sometimes wonder "what if" we had taken the other road. In a poem Robert Frost reflected upon taking "the road less traveled by," and, he said, "that has made all the difference." Sometimes our "what if" is said in regret and longing: if only we had accepted the challenge of some bright opportunity, instead of allowing our timidity to close that door forever.

At other times we look back with satisfaction and give thanks to God that we made the choice we did. "What if," we say with a sigh, "what if I had failed to rise to the moment of my greatest challenge?" An elderly man was relating, with obvious pleasure, some of his many satisfying experiences in his long tenure as the teacher of a young people's class at church school. It hadn't all been fun or easy, and there had been times along the way when he wished he could give it up. But now, as he nears the sunset years of his life, he finds his greatest satisfaction in having taken a hard job and having done it he best he could. Then he added—with a hint of tears in his eyes and voice— "I've often thought of the day when the Sunday School teacher came to ask me to take that class. What if I had said no?" He had learned the secret so many people miss: we get no satisfactions, no victories, no pleasures, no rewards from those opportunities we refuse. It's the things we say yes to that provide us the rich treasures that sustain life and make it enjoyable.

Without doubt Paul relived, many times, that quick decision he made at Troas to forego his plans to go to Bithynia and turn, instead, to the West. In that one tiny choice, the history of the world was changed forever. What if he had said no?

To be sure, his choice would lead to jail in Philippi, a riot in Thessalonica, and a whole catalog of beatings, whippings, trials, a shipwreck, and ultimately to a dungeon in Rome where he would spend the rest of his life. But that momentous decision would also lead to the introduction of the Christian gospel into Europe. What if he had said no?

Every day we face unique opportunities, and the choices we make in facing those challenges may forever alter our destiny.

Be careful how you respond to the opportunities God sets before you today. It might be the "road less traveled" that will make all the difference.

DAY 17
Read Acts 17

When Paul walked into the city of Athens, he could not have helped being impressed by the majestic power of this world center of learning and culture. The acropolis, with its pagan temples, loomed over the city and witnessed to the impregnable religious traditions that held the city in their grip. Surely Paul felt threatened by all the visual evidences of such an entrenched religious establishment. But his qualified successes in Philippi, Beroea, and Thessalonica gave him confidence, despite the fact that he had left his partners Silas and Timothy behind to continue the fledgling work in Berea.

Even Paul's escorts, who led him to Athens, left Paul at the city limits. Surely Paul had never felt so alone.

Nevertheless, Paul went to the marketplace of the city and began to testify to the common people who customarily came there to buy or sell. But some learned philosophers heard of Paul's teaching and invited him to come to the Areopagus to argue his case before the learned men of the city. Paul must have been supremely flattered. Such an opportunity would be like a country preacher being invited to lecture the faculty at Harvard University. And Paul acquitted himself honorably before his learned audience, though his success in Athens was limited. In fact, it might be said with some truth that Athens was the scene of his greatest failure. And there were two reasons for it:

First, Paul left the common folk of the marketplace to devote his attention to the philosophers. Paul's greatest effectiveness was always among the common people, reflecting the ministry of Jesus himself, of whom it was said, "The common people heard him gladly." Leaving the marketplace to go to the Areopagus was surely a mistake that revealed Paul's pride. A second mistake was the fact that instead of offering his own simple testimony, Paul left his familiar territory to argue philosophy with the philosophers. The Christian gospel is best communicated through personal testimony.

It must be conceded that Paul did not leave Athens entirely without converts, but only two are listed: Dionysius the Aeropagite (which means he lived on Philosophers Hill but probably as a servant to the philosophers, who only came there for their daily sessions) and Damaris (a woman, who would never have been admitted to the company of the philosophers). The implication is that none of the philosophers, with whom Paul had exhausted his intellectual appeals, were converted through Paul's teaching.

The lesson for us is clear: We must be ourselves, speaking a language we know, and relating what we have found to be true in our own experience. It is such a witness that encourages others to listen.

DAY 18
Read Acts 18

With a mighty resolve—though surely not without some trepidation—Paul put the city of Athens behind him and headed for Corinth. His meager success in Athens must have been a severe disappointment to him. Of all the earth's capitals, the religiously inclined Athens might have been expected to be the most hospitable to Paul's passionate commitment to tell the world about the new truth that promised new life. But the cynical philosophers replied to Paul with the cruelest of all responses: they yawned.

So Paul left the city of his greatest hope and turned toward the metropolis that was everywhere regarded as the most worldly, least wholesome city on earth. Corinth's reputation was celebrated in a common proverb: "To live like a Corinthian" meant to live a life of conscienceless debauchery.

Add to that dismal prospect the fact that Paul was approaching this grim challenge entirely alone. His missionary partners—Silas and Timothy—had been left behind in Macedonia to continue the new work Paul had established there.

But the first event of Paul's long and productive stay in Corinth was the exciting discovery that he had helpers there who were unknown to him. Aquila and Priscilla, banished from Rome because of their faith, came as a refreshing reminder that God never leaves us comfortless.

The parable that we refer to as "the good Samaritan" suggests many important truths, but none more heartening than this: like the victim of the thieves, lying there wounded beside the road, we can expect some help to come our way. It may not be the help we wanted, and it may not be the help we expected. And the help we expected may fail us. But there will be some help available to us, and it will be exactly the help we need. And whatever human faces or hands may be involved in the process of delivering the help to us, the real source of that help is God. The psalmist asks the question, "From where will my help come?" And the answer is provided, "My help comes from the LORD, who made heaven and earth" (Psalm 121:1–2). And surely the great God, who has the whole creation in the divine pantry of resources, can find some help for you, when you need it and trust God for it.

DAY 19
Read Acts 19

When Paul arrived in Ephesus to begin his missionary work there, he discovered that there were already some disciples living there. How they had come by their knowledge about Christ and the Christian way is not told us. Perhaps a resident of Ephesus had traveled to Antioch or Jerusalem and had heard there of this new movement that was capturing the hearts and lives of so many. Perhaps a letter from a distant relative or friend had introduced them to the Christian faith. What is clear is that their knowledge of the faith was incomplete. But even the small part of the Christian story that came to their hearing invited their response, and they gave evidence of their faith by being baptized.

Much could be said in commendation of those Ephesians, and they certainly put to shame those who refuse to take even the first step to follow the way of the cross until the whole map has been unfolded before them. However complete we assume is our knowledge of the Christian faith now, we must readily concede that our understanding is much more extensive than it was when we began our discipleship. The fact is that Christ meets us wherever we are on the road of spiritual discovery, and the depth of our faith is not measured by how much we know, but how faithful we are in our response to whatever revelation God has chosen to give us.

But there is, at the same time, a sad aspect to limitation of the Ephesian disciples' Christian experience. They had submitted to the baptism as taught and practiced by John the Baptist. It was a baptism of repentance, by which they acknowledged their sinful ways and committed themselves to trying to reform themselves, to "do better" than they had in the past. And as admirable as such efforts are, they certainly do not qualify as "good news," for such efforts are almost always doomed to failure. What they needed was not so much a more honorable intention, but a new source of strength to help them achieve it.

What they needed was the baptism of Christ, in which the Holy Spirit comes into the life of the believer, to provide the means by which good intentions become accomplished deeds.

Never, this side of heaven, will you know everything there is to know about the life to which Christ calls us, but make sure you are faithful to what you know. And don't stop your search for the truth until you have found that gift of grace that makes the Christian life possible.

Dramatic events were swiftly moving toward their inevitable collision as Paul continued his last journey, as a free man, toward Jerusalem. There was iron in his resolve, but something of the tenderness of Paul's sentiment for his friends demanded attention. He could not pass near Ephesus without one last chance to greet those with whom he had worked for three years. So at the port of Miletus, where the River Maeander empties into the Aegean Sea, Paul sent word to Ephesus, asking for the leaders of the church to meet him there for a farewell gathering.

Rarely, in the biographical records of Paul, do we see this tender, sentimental side of the vigorous and courageous apostle. This may have been the first time Paul faced the reality of the dangers that lurked ahead for him. While he did not claim to be able to foresee the events of the future, he was astute enough to assess accurately the perils that awaited him, as he walked into the mouth of the lion of Judah. There must have been a catch in Paul's voice as he told the elders from Ephesus, "Now I know that none of you...will ever see my face again."

But Paul did not want his friends to be anxious about his future, so he shared with them the secret of his equanimity: " I am on my way to Jerusalem," he said, "not knowing what will happen to me there." That sounds like a recipe for anxiety. But listen as Paul completes that thought: "...except that the Holy Spirit testifies to me in every city" (vv. 22–23). Paul had an unfailing advocate, a friend in high places, an unfailing guarantor. What he knew was greater than what he did not know.

During the Second World War, a London woman always managed to sleep soundly through the nightly bombing raids that ravaged the city and claimed many lives. Once she was asked the secret of her calm. "Well," she replied, "I Read   in the Bible that the Lord who keeps me will neither slumber nor sleep. So I say, what's the use of the both of us staying awake?"

While few of us can evidence such complete trust, there is no doubt that when we view the future in companionship with God, we have a truer picture of the resources with which we will greet the days to come.

DAY 21
Read Acts 21

Contrasting sharply with Paul's emotional farewell to the Ephesian elders, Paul gave scant attention to the mournful warnings of a prophet named Agabus. It was in the city of Caesarea, where Paul's voyage to Judea ended. He stayed in the home of Philip, one of the original deacons. Perhaps Paul was enjoying a few days of rest before continuing to Jerusalem. But while he was at Philip's house, a prophet named Agabus appeared before him and warned him of impending dangers that the apostle would face if he completed his plan by going to Jerusalem.

The weeping prophet's admonitions set off a torrent of sorrow from Paul's friends, who urged him not to go to Jerusalem in the light of such peril. Even Luke, in writing the account of this scene, included himself among those who tried to dissuade Paul. But the apostle's reply was resolute: "What are you doing, weeping and breaking my heart? For I am ready not only to be bound but even to die in Jerusalem for the name of the Lord Jesus" (v. 13)

In his response to those who would shield Paul from such dangers, he shows the same spirit as Jesus, who once rebuffed Peter for such well-intended protectiveness: "Get behind me, Satan! You are a stumbling block to me, for you are setting your mind not on divine things but on human things" (Matthew 16:23). Paul faced a similar peril as he set his face to go to Jerusalem. And as much as it would exact from him, he knew that the glory was where the danger was.

As much as we might wish it otherwise, Christian discipleship often demands sacrifice of us. It ought to say something to us that the symbol of the Christian faith is a rugged cross and not a rocking chair. And those who would seek to dissuade us from costly dedication and heroic acts are not our friends.

Teresa of Avila is credited with the little prayer, "Lord, protect me from my friends; I can protect myself from my enemies."

Beware of those who might, in their solicitude, endeavor to pamper you by removing the bumps from your path of life. The bumps are what you climb on.

DAY 22
Read Acts 22

There are, in everyone's life, days of such decisive importance that they spring to memory in any later review of one's experiences. Often such days receive their gravity from our own actions. At other times such a day derives its solemnity from events that befall us, and how we react to them. And sometimes we do not recognize the solemnity of such a day as we are living it, but only when, in retrospect, we can see how the contents of that day set a new course or gave birth to a new purpose. But all of us can see, as we look across the landscape of our past, those peaks of joy or sorrow, good or evil, fortune or loss that gave a new interpretation to the past and a new purpose for the future.

Surely Paul, in years to come, would list this day of his entry into Jerusalem as such a pivotal and life-changing time. When the day began, did he have any knowledge–or even an inkling–that before the day ended he would be wearing the chains from which he would never again be free? Would he have passed that point of no return? Like the Christ for whom he now lived, his entry into Jerusalem would cut off all alternatives but the one that was his constant motive: "It is no longer I who live, but it is Christ who lives in me" (Galatians 2:20). And if that was truly the raison d'être of his life, going to Jerusalem was exactly the right thing for him to do, for that decision set Paul's footsteps on a path that would lead him to the most monumental contribution to the Christian faith ever made by a human being. He would surely spend the rest of his life in jail, but from those prison bars would escape the epistles that teach us most of what we know about Christian theology. And likewise from those prison cells sprang forth the spirit of Christian love that would conquer even the mighty Roman Empire.

As Paul was later to report to his Philippian Christian friends (from a prison cell), "I want you to know, beloved, that what has happened to me has actually helped to spread the gospel" (Philippians 1:12). Neither prison bars nor beatings, neither shipwrecks nor tempests, neither perfidious friends nor bloodthirsty enemies could conquer that spirit of Paul, or diminish the joy it gave him, for on that pivotal day in Jerusalem he chose to seek the peace that the world can neither give nor take away. And what he gave that day was dwarfed by what he would receive, from that day forever.

DAY 23
Read Acts 23

The story of Paul's life, as Luke reported it in the book of Acts, at times resembles the old movie serials of the 1930s and 1940s, with the hero faced, at regular intervals, with calamities from which no escape seems possible. But–like those old serials again–Paul's salvation frequently came from some unexpected source.

A case in point is the conspiracy of a group of Jewish men who took an oath that they would neither eat nor drink until they had killed Paul, thus dusting their hands of this threat to their ecclesiastical status quo. Though it is not a principal emphasis of this story, it is worth noting that, contrary to our frequent opinion, the validity of one's religious belief cannot be measured by the sacrificial commitment of its adherents. The extreme sacrifices exacted from their members by the cults remind us of this fallacy. The tragedy is that we are so often satisfied with the meager commitment of many to what is surely the truth of God. Think what God could do with such commitment as we see demonstrated in the oath of Paul's enemies!

But shining like a brilliant gem in the midst of this story is the salvation of Paul from a most unlikely source. Who knew that Paul had a sister? Or that she had a son? Or that this nephew of Paul's lived in Jerusalem? Or that this hitherto unknown relative of Paul's was "tuned in" to the frequency of God's will, and would be willing and able to represent God's grace in rescuing Paul? Does it sound like that old Tarzan serial, with certain death averted with the help of a previously unknown source? More than that, it sounds like the persistence of a loving and faithful God, who may search through a warehouse full of resources before finding the very help that will answer your prayer.

Many who are now older adults can remember a picture that was popular in the time of their childhood, and that may, in fact, have hung over their bed. It depicts two children who are walking across a bridge, one floor plank of which has been broken out. The children are walking with carefree inattention, never suspecting what possible peril confronts them. But unseen to them (but not to us) is the angel who goes before them, guiding their steps, to make it possible for them to walk over the bridge in safety, never knowing the calamity that they avoided because of the angel's care.

Not alone for children, but for all of us is the assurance that "he will command his angels concerning you, to guard you in all your ways" (Psalm 91:11).

Between the memorable events of Paul's ministry that shine like lighthouses along the shore of time, there were often long intervals when nothing of consequence seemed to be going on. Paul's dramatic nighttime transfer from Jerusalem to Caesarea was followed by two years of imprisonment, in which there was nothing to report, except for two disheartening trials before a petty functionary of the Roman empire. And though Paul poured out his heart and soul in these brief interviews with Felix, nothing of substance seems to have resulted from them. How could Paul have endured such a forced retirement from his missionary endeavors, when there was still a whole world to win for Christ? What a waste of those two years!

But perhaps they were not a waste, after all. Although we have no specific knowledge of Paul's activities during this two-year furlough from his missionary service, we can extrapolate, from what we know about Paul's earlier and later times of imprisonment, that important events occurred in that prison cell. Who can guess what congregations Paul instructed and inspired through letters he wrote from that prison?

Although we have only thirteen letters in the New Testament canon that are believed to have been written by Paul, there is strong evidence that Paul wrote many others that have not survived. And it is entirely possible that Paul's greatest contribution to the church came through his written word.

We may certainly conclude that Paul spent much of his time behind bars in prayer. He frequently told his Christian friends that he was praying for them. Unless that was an empty and insincere flaunting of superficial piety, Paul had to spend a considerable amount of time redeeming those spiritual IOU's.

And he surely spent a great amount of time thinking the deep thoughts of God. Paul's earlier epistles (1 and 2 Thessalonians, for example) fall far short of matching the majesty of thought evident in his later letters (like Romans and Ephesians). Obviously, Paul had studied much and meditated deeply upon the faith that had claimed him. In fact, it is possible that without those frequent times of imprisonment, Paul would not have become the chief architect of the theology of the Christian faith.

Is it possible that your times of greatest growth and contribution may come when little of consequence seems to be happening in your life?

Jesus' frightening prophecy had come to pass. In preparing his disciples for the difficulties they would face, Jesus said, "You will be dragged before governors and kings because of me"" (Matthew 10:18). Jesus himself faced such a fate, when he was dragged into the imperial presence of Governor Pilate, and paraded before the royal attention of King Herod. In both of those trials, the judge thought more of his own popularity than of the victim who stood before him.

Now the scene is the same, but other actors have assumed the major roles.

Instead of Jesus, Paul is the accused prisoner in the dock. In Herod's place is King Agrippa, the figurehead king of the Jews, who owed his position to the Roman government, and was likely to keep his crown only as long as he kept his subjects under control. The real political authority here, a successor of Pilate, is the governor, Festus. Like his predecessor in that position, Festus was a just man who took seriously his mandate to govern fairly, but he was also responsible for keeping the peace among a populace of Jews who needed little provocation to turn their resentment against Rome into armed rebellion. So as Paul was "dragged before governors and kings" because of Christ, he knew that each of his judges would be supremely interested in how their judgment would affect their own lives.

As vigorously as we may condemn such self-serving judgments, it is nevertheless true that our choices always affect us more profoundly than anyone else. History records that Pilate spent his last years haunted by his failure to defend the Christ whom he clearly saw to be innocent. Herod Antipas, unable to retain the favor of the Roman establishment, was banished by Caligula to Gaul, where he died.

Whatever good may have been done by those governors and kings, history's judgment says only that faced with an opportunity to defend the right, they missed their chance, and spent the rest of their days imprisoned in the shadow of their failure.

The irony is that it was not Jesus who was on trial when he stood before those petty potentates. As history affirms, it was his judges who were on trial.

Nor is Christ on trial before our scanty allegiance; but it shocks us to realize who is on trial.

DAY 26
Read Acts 26

As he stood before King Agrippa and Governor Festus that day, Paul knew that his defense of the Christian faith would have to be eminently persuasive and intellectually sound. Furthermore, Paul surely saw this encounter as an opportunity to contend for the souls of two men who, despite their political importance, were still children of God for whom Christ died. Paul would be capable of debating the philosophical concepts underlying the Christian ethic, or the great theological bases of the gospel. But Paul chose, instead, to offer his own personal witness of how Christ had loved him and pursued him and brought him into the kingdom of God.

It was a story that Paul knew well, for he had told it again and again, before multitudes of people, and privately for individual seekers. His story was a microcosm of the miracle of redemption: something done by God through Christ, and Paul's own response to that good news. It was, in point of fact, the whole story of the Christian faith. And every Christian must have his own version of that story, and must be able to see through it the entire meaning of the gospel.

After describing that seminal event on the Damascus Road, in which he was confronted by a blinding vision of the Christ, Paul summed up his response by saying, "I was not disobedient to the heavenly vision." Everything Paul had done as a Christian evangelist, missionary, and theologian could be described as being obedient to the heavenly vision. He had seen something that deserved his obedience, and he gladly gave it. "I was not disobedient to the heavenly vision."

Though few if any of us will have such a dramatic experience as that heavenly vision of Paul's, we all have those moments when we can see the truth more clearly than on most days. There are those clear days of inspiration and deeply felt conviction that turn our hearts and our footsteps resolutely toward some worthy goal. There are those episodes in life in which life's meaning becomes crystal clear, and we revise our agendas to give primacy to what the vision has shown us. But then there come those days when clouds of doubt and confusion obscure the vision that once set our feet to marching and our hearts to singing, and we are tempted to question the validity of what we saw on that clear day.

But on such days, let us remember the strategy of Paul, who "was not disobedient to the heavenly vision." Our faith is perfected not when we can see the vision of God's truth, but when we remember that vision and follow it even when we can't.

DAY 27
Read Acts 27

It has frequently been observed that in times of calamity or peril, qualities of character emerge that have previously been unrealized. A "bumper sticker" axiom expresses this truth: "Christians are like tea bags: their real strength comes out in hot water." And if ever a Christian was in hot water, it was certainly Paul, during that crucial voyage toward Rome.

As a result of Paul's request, as a Roman citizen, to stand before Caesar to have his case reviewed, he was delivered into the charge of a Roman centurion named Julius.

Also in the company were Paul's friend and missionary partner, Luke, and Aristarchus, a Macedonian Christian who had been a follower and helper of Paul's ever since his conversion in Thessalonica. The first leg of the voyage was on a small ship that called only at ports of Asia Minor. But at the port city of Myra in Lycia the centurion booked passage for himself and his little company aboard a grain ship from Egypt bound for Rome. It was on that second ship that a ferocious tempest descended upon the little company.

On that ill-fated voyage–begun, against Paul's advice, too late in the autumn to be assured of fair weather–there was a company of two hundred seventy-six souls. The logical leader would have been the captain of the ship, although Julius, the centurion, might have exercised the privilege of his high rank to assume control. But strangely, it was Paul, the prisoner, to whom the company looked for direction and comfort. Paul emerged as a leader worth following because he was following a leader worth following. At the blackest and bleakest of times, Paul announced to the ship's company, "Keep up your courage, men, for I have faith in God..."

What a burden of responsibility Paul assumed on his shoulders, offering his faith as reason for others to hope! And in the excruciating hours and days to come, the people aboard that ship clung to Paul's faith as if it were a life preserver–as, indeed, it was.

Too little has been made of this social responsibility of a Christian's faith. It is not enough that our faith saves us: we must assume responsibility for the saving of others as well.

The challenge each of us faces is this: Who is being drawn into the kingdom of God by our faith?

DAY 28
Read Acts 28

Who has not come to the last page of a book that has been thoroughly enjoyed, with a feeling of sadness that there was not one more chapter or at least one more page to enjoy? And despite Luke's careful record, we are left with several questions that a comprehensive biography would answer.

After a brilliant career as a missionary and builder of churches, Paul had, at last, come to the city that was the capital of the world: Rome. But did he fulfill that burning ambition to stand before Caesar to argue his case for the Christian faith? As a Roman citizen he was guaranteed that right, but Luke is strangely silent on the subject. One cannot imagine that Paul would sanguinely accept a denial of the opportunity that he had long cherished, and for which he had endured incarceration, a tempest, a shipwreck, and various other vicissitudes. And what a scene that would have been, with Paul at last standing before Caesar, and Caesar confronted by someone who cared more for his eternal soul than for all the earthly power that he represented. But if such a confrontation occurred, we are not informed of it.

And Luke's strange conclusion, which reveals to us that Paul "lived there two whole years at his own expense," begs the question of what happened at the end of those two years. Was Paul released after those two years, perhaps to continue his missionary travels, maybe at last to go to Spain, which he had longed to do? Or did those two years in Rome end with Paul's death? Paul's declining strength and health leave us to surmise that his last written words to Timothy may have been fulfilled, "The time of my departure has come. I have fought the good fight, I have finished the race, I have kept the faith" (2 Timothy 4:6–7).

But perhaps the question is moot, for Paul lived by the conviction that if he did, in each day as it came, the thing that Christ led him to do, he would not need to be anxious about the future. In fact, Paul seemed very casual about his future, reminding his Christian friends at Philippi, "For to me, living is Christ and dying is gain. If I am to live in the flesh, that means fruitful labor for me; and I do not know which I prefer" (Philippians 1:21–22).

But surely Paul found both quiet peace and radiant joy in the fact that his last two years gave him opportunity to witness to his Lord, and to continue his discipleship unhindered. And whatever came at the end of that time, it was a blessing.

DAY 29
Read Romans 1

When the occasion prescribed it, Paul was capable of shaking the floorboards with his thunderous rhetoric, reducing his recalcitrant hearers to cringing children. That was especially true of Paul's writings to churches he had established and toward which he felt a certain understandable paternalism. But in his letter to Rome—where he had never been—and to the church there—which he had no hand in planting—Paul was the soul of gallantry.

A lovely example of this is Paul's statement in verses eleven and twelve of the first chapter of the Roman epistle. As the divinely appointed apostle to the Gentiles, and as the church's chief spokesman, he might have felt a certain authority to speak dogmatically to the Christians living in the shadow of Caesar's palace, but listen to his gentle urbanity: "I am longing to see you so that I may share with you some spiritual gift to strengthen you—or rather so that we may be mutually encouraged by each other's faith, both yours and mine."

How it must have strengthened their faith to hear the great apostle say that they had something to teach him! And how it must have prepared their hearts to receive what Paul had to offer them! His attitude is reminiscent of Isaiah's prophecy, which Matthew applied to Jesus: "He will not break a bruised reed or quench a smoldering wick" (Matthew 12:20). Jesus honored a centurion for his rudimentary faith, and praised a widow for her tiny offering, and allowed a Samaritan woman to give him a drink. In doing so, he honored each one and recognized that they had something to give that was worth receiving.

Not only is this gallantry an essential element of any successful effort to help anyone, but also it helps us to understand the universal truth that everyone knows something we need to learn and has something we need to receive. And the most effective Christian teachers are not those whose attitude says, "I have something you need: take it," but rather those whose bearing conveys the understanding that we can find more good if we search for it together.

In this attitude we see again the underlying philosophy of the Christian faith that honors every person as someone created in the image of God, and for whom Christ died. It is in this understanding that we discover that God may use anyone as a channel through which God speaks to us some word we need to hear.

It has been said that God's qualities are so beyond the reach of human expression that mere words are like drops of water attempting to describe the ocean. And while the greatness of God makes that a true statement, it must also be observed that while a single drop of water is most assuredly not the whole ocean, it would be false to say that that one drop is not ocean! And while that one drop, minute as it is, can hardly suffice to inform us of all the permutations assumed by the ocean in various places and circumstances, it still contains one part of oxygen to two parts of hydrogen as its basic composition, which is true of the whole ocean everywhere.

So Paul selects three qualities to attribute to God, and while each is certainly a benevolent quality, they seem a bit like drops of water attempting to define the ocean: "kindness, forbearance and patience." Does that sound a bit like damning with faint praise? Surely more impressive verbiage might have been enlisted for so magnificent a task! Don't we want a God who is more than kind, more than forbearing, more than patient?

But despite the devaluation of our language that has resulted from our inflated usage, kindness, forbearance, and patience are ultimate expressions of love that cannot be earned, cannot be measured, and cannot be defeated.

Kindness is love that never asks, "How much?" or whether its extravagances are deserved. Forbearance is forgiveness that keeps turning the other cheek, even when the blows show no sign of stopping. Patience is honoring the supreme value of someone who does not even value her- or himself.

The fact that God is kind must be understood as the result of God's intentional choice. The fact that God does not punish us is no indication that God cannot punish us. It is as if God has made each of us, individually, an offer of executive clemency. We do not earn such divine kindness. We can only accept it, and be grateful for it, and live in expression of the joy that radiates from such a gift.

DAY 31
Read Romans 3

There is a kind of noblesse oblige that every Christian must accept as a necessary consequence of the privilege of receiving God's grace. In writing to the Roman Christians, Paul was aware of the controversy that raged throughout the church with regard to any special privilege that God might have conferred upon the Jews. As a former leader and teacher of the Jewish faith, Paul was admirably equipped to discuss the matter. And though Paul made it quite clear that Gentiles had the same access to God as the Jews, he still conceded that the Jews had some advantages that the Gentiles lacked.

Principally, the Jews had learned the "oracles of God"–the Ten Commandments and other teachings of the Old Testament.

But did such a gift imply special privilege? No, but it did confer upon the Jews a special responsibility. Paul's consistent teaching throughout his writings is that God gives to us so that we may have something to give others. And every benefaction God confers upon us, and that we can list as among our assets, must be accounted for by some acknowledgment of responsibility on the liability side.

With such sublime endowments as the Law, the Prophets, and the millennia of history in divine-human interaction, the Jews should have been especially prepared and ready to accept the Lordship of Jesus Christ. But their privilege became a roadblock to many Jews who were unable to move beyond their past to see God's future. So their privilege became a curse instead of a blessing.

Most of us present-day Christians are the most richly blessed people who ever lived. God has given us the Holy Word, which others wrote, preserved, translated, and conveyed, often at great cost to themselves. We have the church that was built by other hands and defended against heresy and persecution by the godliest of earth's men and women. We have been granted a historical setting in which our faith is neither condemned nor discouraged. What must God expect of us, in the stewardship of such wealth?

Like the Jews of Paul's day, we have apparently been singled out for special privilege, in order that we might fulfill special responsibility. What will you do today, to justify such generosity?

It is so difficult for us logical human beings to understand that God does not deal with us on a quid pro quo, tit-for-tat basis. Such an approach overestimates the value of our contribution to God, and underestimates God's delightful proclivity for going beyond what we deserve. That was the problem with the Jewish concept of justification by works, which contends that we earn God's blessing by our meticulous obedience to the laws of God. But there are two problems with that belief. First, there is no one, however sincerely motivated, who can claim to be 100 percent obedient to God. As hard as we may try, we will always fail in some manner, and will, therefore, find that instead of being our defender, the law has become our accuser.

But a second problem with this concept of justification by works is that it puts the favor of God within the reach of human payment. It cheapens the grace of God to the level of a bribe. Instead, keeping the laws of God ought to be seen as following the directions God has given us to find the happiest, most productive life.

God's favor is entirely disconnected from that mathematical formula. Grace comes as the surprising gift of God that gives us open and uncluttered access to all the riches of God, whether we have been obedient to God's laws or not. And that gift is not related to our obedience, but rather to our trust. Understood in that way, obeying the law is really something we do for ourselves. Trust is what we do that opens our lives to the favor of God.

A whimsical story tells of a minister who died and appeared before Saint Peter to be judged for his worthiness to enter heaven. When the saint asked the applicant what claim he had on heaven's glory, he answered, "For more than fifty years I was a minister." "Good!" replied Saint Peter. "That's one point. You need one hundred points to enter here." "Well," the minister continued, "I Read   my Bible and prayed every day, and gave a tithe of my income to God." "Good," the saint said, "that's one more point. You still need ninety-eight." "I called on the sick and shut-ins, and cared for the troubled, and counseled with the confused." "Excellent," said Peter. "That's a grand total of three points. You still need ninety-seven to get in here."

"Ninety-seven more points? I'll never have enough points! Without the grace of God I'd never make it." And the saint closed his account book and said, "Oh, the grace of God! That's different. That's worth exactly ninety-seven points. Come on in!"

However far your efforts and labors may leave you from heaven's gate, the unearnable, undeservable, unexpectable grace of God gives you just what you need.

DAY 33
Read Romans 5

Here, in the fifth chapter of the letter to the Romans, is one of those luminous passages of which Paul was eminently capable, in which he presents some of the deepest thoughts of Christian theology in pungently memorable expressions. Like a symphony it begins by stating the theme ("Since we are justified by faith, we have peace with God through our Lord Jesus Christ" [v. 1]). Then through variations on the theme he shows how this primary fact of our salvation through Christ lights up every aspect of life. What a difference it makes when we have found this "peace with God."

One of the variations concerns our troubles. Unfortunately, our Christian faith does not immunize us against difficulties and sufferings, any more than Paul was exempt from the slings and arrows of outrageous fortune. But Paul's relationship with God gave him a strategy for turning those vicissitudes into blessings.

Someone once attempted to commiserate with a woman of deep faith who was undergoing a time of extreme difficulty by saying, "Tribulations do so color life, don't they?" And the gallant soul replied, "Indeed they do. And with God's help I will choose the color!"

So Paul was able to say that he gloried in his sufferings, not because he was a masochist who enjoyed pain and problems, but because with the set of his soul, the winds of adversity served only to blow him toward his ultimate goal. "[My] suffering produces endurance, and endurance produces character, and character produces hope, and hope does not disappoint us" (vv. 3–5a). Was that reasoning only the baseless claims of rose-colored Pollyannaism? Certainly not, because Paul concludes that statement by saying "because God's love has been poured into our hearts through the Holy Spirit that has been given to us."

It was that same spirit that Jesus expressed on the cross when he said, "Father, into your hands I commend my spirit" (Luke 23:46). The word "commend" is a translation of the original Greek word, *paratheke,* which was a banking term meaning "deposit." Jesus did not fear the rigors of the crucifixion or the terrors of death, because he had deposited his real treasure—his eternal soul—into the safe hands of God.

DAY 34
Read Romans 6

‘Oscar Wilde was quoted as saying, "Life is admirably arranged: I love to sin and God loves to forgive."

Apparently there were those in the fellowship of Roman Christians who inclined toward Wilde's understanding. If God delighted in forgiving sinners, why not keep on giving God the pleasure that produces such delight? The more we sin, the more God has the opportunity to exercise the attribute that is the most godly—which is grace—and the more grace we receive.

But Paul quickly puts that reasoning to rest by affirming that it is inexcusably blasphemous to use God's mercy as an excuse to sin. And furthermore, when one becomes a Christian, he or she no longer looks for loopholes that might provide an opportunity to sin. In dramatic terms, Paul says that we are dead to sin. Sin no longer has dominion over us.

Does that mean, then, that as Christians we will no longer be tempted to sin? Unfortunately, that is not the case, as Paul will clearly affirm in the next chapter of this epistle. But once we have found peace with God through Jesus Christ, and have received the gift of the Holy Spirit to dwell within us, we have a new incentive, a new motivation, and a new power by which to deny the dominance of sin.

An old country preacher was trying to express this difficult concept of the contest between good and evil that is constantly being waged within us. He said, "There are two dogs inside me—a good dog and a bad dog, and they are always snarling at each other and threatening each other. Each one wants to win, and each one expects to win."

A hearer asked him, "And which dog wins?" And the preacher replied, "Whichever one I say 'sic-em' to."

So becoming a Christian doesn't deprive us of our divinely given right of moral choice. Each of us has the freedom of will that allows us to say "yes" or "no" to every choice that confronts us. Jesus recognized that, and to Peter in the Upper Room (who Jesus knew would be sorely tempted to betray his Lord before the night was over) our Lord said, "Simon, Simon, listen! Satan has demanded to sift all of you like wheat, but I have prayed for you that your own faith may not fail" (Luke 22:31–32). On the stage of our souls there is a constant and crucial debate: Satan demands us, and Christ prays for us. And who wins? Whoever we say "sic-em" to.

Some Bible scholars believe Paul's reference to "this body of death" draws its meaning from a particularly cruel form of punishment in which one judged to be guilty of a grievous offense was chained–wrist to wrist and ankle to ankle–with the dead body of another evildoer. The guilty could never escape the reminder of his own mortality, and his every thought and deed was dominated by it. It is not a pleasant picture to contemplate, but it does define Paul's feeling about the penalty imposed by the flesh upon the spirit.

We must question Paul's revulsion toward the physical aspect of life, for although the body and everything it represents are temporary and subject to inevitable decay, the flesh is, after all, the vehicle of the spirit for as long as we live in this world. And through the functions of the flesh we come to know God and serve God. But Paul's rather excessive condemnation of the physical body probably resulted from his frustration that even as seasoned and accomplished a Christian as he was, there was that last stubborn inch of resistance and rebellion that kept him from perfect obedience.

The principal reminder to us here is the unavoidable fact that we are split personalities from the moment of our birth until we draw our last breath. We are both soul and body, and every one of us must decide whether we are primarily a body temporarily possessing a soul, or whether we are essentially a soul temporarily residing in a body. And we choose the nature we want to be by giving it our attention and nurturing it.

When an astronaut leaves the space capsule to take a "space walk," he knows that he has come into a world that is hostile to him. He cannot live in that environment without the attention and support provided by the "umbilical cord" that keeps him attached to his spacecraft. That umbilical cord serves three purposes: it keeps him from getting lost, it provides him the oxygen that he needs in order to survive, and it provides a means of communication with the world that has given him life.

So our bodies are of this world. They are perfectly at home here, and, as a part of this world, will share the destiny of all earthly things. But our souls belong to God. And unless we remain in contact with God, our souls cannot survive.

Edgar DeWitt Jones, one of America's greatest preachers in the early days of the twentieth century, called it "The Matterhorn of the Holy Scriptures." By that sobriquet he was referring to the last twelve verses of the eighth chapter of Romans. The Matterhorn is, of course, the majestic peak that rises dramatically from the Swiss landscape, like a cyclopean signboard left by some earlier race of giants, to point its unmistakable way to heaven. At its base are numerous other hills of the Alps, but this autograph of the Creator's art dwarfs them all.

So in his epistle to the Romans, for all its profound delving into matters of immense theological importance, Paul suddenly comes to a clearing and lifts up his eyes in wonder to one of the most glorious insights to be found in holy writ. Behind him, now, are all those frustrations of the endless contest between spirit and flesh. Lain aside, for the moment, are all those logical but tedious considerations about the law. Now, occupying Paul's entire view— and ours—is that glorious truth that brings all life together into a radiant realization: "We know that all things work together for good for those who love God, who are called according to his purpose" (v. 28).

Wait a minute, Paul! What about war? That's surely not a good thing, and no rose-colored glasses can make it look good. And what about cancer, and human hunger, and hatred between brothers and sisters in the human family? Surely not all things are good. But that is not what Paul says. All things are not good. Is Paul guilty, here, of a superficial but groundless optimism? No, Paul was stating the truth that he had, himself, discovered: When we are on the right path, headed toward the right destination, everything that happens to us can be utilized to bring us toward our goal.

Calamities that might have utterly defeated someone else worked together for Paul's good, because he loved God, and was fulfilling holy purposes with his life.

It has been said that God can mend a broken heart, if you give God all the pieces.

And if you give God your whole life, the Creator can use everything that comes to you—even the worst calamities—as materials for the building of your life of blessing.

A small-town politician once met a minister who was well known for his preaching on predestination and fore-ordination, and about those who will be among the elect in heaven. The politician, who did not share the preacher's theology, engaged him in a sidewalk debate. "Preacher," the politician said, "I hear you often preach on predestination and about those who will be among the elect. But tell me, do you think I will be one of the elect?"

The preacher paused before making this reply: "Well, you once ran for city council, and you got elected to that. Then you ran for mayor and got elected to that. Now you ask me if I think you will be among the elect in heaven. But I don't see how you can get elected to something you're not running for."

While few of us subscribe to the Calvinist view of predestination—which asserts that God decides our eternal fate before we are born, and nothing we can do will change that verdict—there is a truth in Calvin's teaching that we must not miss. Salvation is the free and unearned gift of God. Nothing we are capable of doing can purchase forgiveness of our sins. No works of compassion or reverence can give us the right to confront God with the demand: "I earned your grace, now give it to me."

Nevertheless, there are fruits of repentance and faith that we can produce that make us capable of receiving God's gift. But however important are those signs that God is looking for in our lives, they still do not give us the right to assume that we have thereby earned God's favor.

So with profound sorrow Paul laments the tragedy of the Jews whom God favored with extraordinary privilege, but whose rejection of God's gift disqualified them from receiving it. On the contrary, the Gentiles whom God had not favored with special opportunities showed the faith and obedience that God honored with the divine gift of redemption.

Perhaps it is an oversimplification (and one must never trivialize God's amazing grace), but can we say, at the most elementary level of understanding this profound truth, that although our "running for" election to heaven cannot get us there, neither can we get elected to something we aren't running for?

DAY 38

The Bible contains many anthropomorphic pictures of God (that is, images that ascribe to God human qualities). All such images must necessarily be flawed, since God is far beyond human comparison in every respect. They do, however, suggest truths we can know about God. Some of these human images hint at the power of God, or the justice of God, or the omniscience of God. But none are more beautiful than those that see God as a loving and long-suffering parent who grieves over a rebellious and disobedient child. One of the most beautiful of these references is in Hosea, in which God pleads with Israel, as if the nation were a rebellious and intractable child. And God says tearfully,

> "How can I give you up, Ephraim?
> How can I hand you over, O Israel?...
> My heart recoils within me." (Hosea 11:8)

Like the father in Jesus' parable of the prodigal son, God is seen as agonizing over lost children, begging them to return, and waiting patiently, sorrowfully, until they turn their footsteps in God's direction again.

So Paul recalls a similar picture of God from Isaiah:

> "I held out my hands all day long to a rebellious people,
> who walk in a way that is not good." (Isaiah 65:2)

Think of the eternal God, suffering over your rebellion, reaching out hands to you—not fists gripped tight in anger and vengeance, but hands open in pleading and invitation, hands freely offering gifts. That is the God Paul wanted the Jews to see, and that we must see, as well, when there is yet in us any rebellion, any disobedience, any rejection of God's will for us.

The astonishing fact is that God, who possesses all the powers in the universe, chooses to pursue us with sacrificial love, rather than with controlling force. When we fight against God's will for our lives, it isn't so much a matter of breaking God's laws as it is a matter of breaking God's heart.

DAY 39

Two adolescent girls were talking, and the subject was boys. One of them said to the other, about a lad with whom she had broken up: "I have completely gotten over him. In fact, I haven't given him a single thought for three days, fourteen hours, and seventeen minutes." Such was Paul's frequently repeated assertion that the Jews had lost their favored position with God because of their rejection of Christ.

Why did Paul find it so difficult to lay this tragedy to rest and move on in his ministry to the Gentiles? Perhaps it was because Paul was himself a Jew, and must have counted many friends and family members among those quickly and neatly labeled "Jews." Stereotypes are always cruel and unjust, and fail to recognize that every person is a unique child of God. Maybe Paul's inability to settle this matter in his own mind was his memory of many Jewish people—like his old teacher Gamaliel—who were pious, sincere, and righteous people. How could Paul be content with an ethnic judgment that failed to consider the attributes that made each a cherished creation of a loving God?

But surely there was a deeper reason for Paul's reluctance to let go of the tragedy of the rejection of the Christ by many Jews: even if the Jews rejected God, God would not reject them. If God is God, the same divine qualities will be evident in all God's dealings with everyone, all the time. God will never be less than absolute grace, even toward those who spit in his face.

An apocryphal story tells of Judas Iscariot, after that betrayer of Christ committed suicide. His soul wandered through the barren, limitless regions between heaven and hell. Heaven would not accept him; even hell refused him entrance. Earth refused to take him back.

Finally Judas saw, through the clear, cold night of eternal nothingness, a cabin, with illuminated windows. Smoke curling from the chimney gave evidence of a warming fire. Judas rushed toward the door, but in his exhaustion he fell in the snow just before reaching it. That door suddenly swung open, revealing the cheery warmth of the interior of the cabin. And opening the door was the Risen Christ, who said, "Come in, Judas, come in! I was expecting you, and I was just waiting for you before pouring the wine."

It is the nature of that love that it will not let us go.

It was characteristic of Paul's letters that after exploring theological profundities, he would turn his attention to practical matters. He knew that his readers had to live in a real world, and had to live out their Christian faith within the confines of ordinary human existence. But Paul makes it clear that such practical applications of our faith is not incidental to our understanding of the Christian life, but is, indeed, the very essence of our discipleship.

Let us remember, too, that Paul was addressing people who were accustomed to witnessing human sacrifices. In pagan cultures such acts were regarded as the supreme proof of one's devotion and a testimony to the importance of the religion such a sacrifice honored.

But our God is the Lord of mercy, and it was in the name of that mercy that Paul appealed to his readers to give themselves, not as dead sacrifices, but as living gifts to God. Paul specifically appealed to his "brothers and sisters" to present their bodies to God. That would have been a shocking statement to people schooled in the culture of the Greek philosophers, who believed that the body was evil, and that no good could come from it. They believed that the body was only a prison for the soul.

But that was never the Christian view. Rather, the body is seen as the temple of the Holy Spirit, and is capable of serving God, just as the soul is. In fact, without the body the soul would be incapable of giving to God the service God asks. Paul says that giving our bodies in God's service is no less than spiritual worship.

So the apostle lays down the conviction that the church is not the only place we go to worship God (though the New Testament does, indeed, commend that essential practice), but that we can also go to work to worship God, or go home to our families to worship God, or go to help a neighbor in distress to worship God.

In so doing, we are discerning for ourselves–and demonstrating to others–that the good and acceptable and perfect will of God is to show our love for God by loving those whom God loves, and giving our hands and feet to make that worthy aim more than a sentimental thought.

DAY 41
Read Romans 13

In his Confessions, St. Augustine relates the story of his conversion to the Christian faith. He had been given the priceless heritage of a loving Christian mother, Monica, who made it the chief burden of her prayers to lead her son to the faith. But Augustine was a hot-blooded youth who pursued the pleasures of the flesh with great abandon. His appetites and ambitions finally led him to Italy, far from his mother's immediate influence. But her prayers followed him even to that faraway place.

Occasionally Augustine attempted to live according to the Christian principles he had observed in his mother's life, but having no help beyond himself, he was unable to achieve that life of Christian discipleship. One day he was in his garden with his friend, Alypius, a Christian. Augustine was distressed—torn between his desires to be a Christian and his inescapable urges to live contrary to the teachings of Christ. In his torment, he cried aloud, "How long? How long must I delay coming to Christ, to put an end to my depravity?"

Then it was almost as though someone else put new words into his mouth: words that declared, "Why not now? Why not this hour and this moment to put an end to my rebellion against God?" And suddenly he heard a voice saying, "Take and read." He went to the place where his friend Alypus was sitting, and found there a book that his friend had been reading. It was a book of Paul's writings. He read the first words he saw, and they were these words from the thirteenth chapter of Romans: "You know what time it is, how it is now the moment for you to wake from sleep. For salvation is nearer to us now than when we became believers; the night is far gone, the day is near. Let us then lay aside the works of darkness and put on the armor of light; let us live honorably as in the day, not in reveling and drunkenness, not in debauchery and licentiousness, not in quarrelling and jealousy. Instead, put on the Lord Jesus Christ..." (13:11–14). And in the inspiration of that moment, he gave his heart to Christ.

That portion of the scriptures should be underlined in every Bible and imprinted on every heart, for it gave us one of the most devout and challenging of the saints.

You know at least one thing you ought to do to bring your life more into conformity with the will of God and to make some contribution to the kingdom that God has specifically equipped you to make. How long before you wake up and take that step? Why not this hour and this minute?

DAY 42
Read Romans 14

Despite the passage of two millennia and the multitude of changes that have taken place in that span, the picture Paul paints of the church in the first century bears a striking resemblance to the fellowship of believers we all know very well in this age. The church was—and is—composed of human beings who have their own strengths and weaknesses, their own gifts and faults, and the church is made both richer and more disquieted by the contributions of each.

On the Day of Pentecost, when the church was born, it was said that the disciples were "all together in one place" (the King James Version says "in one accord") (Acts 2:1). But if the followers of Christ had somehow achieved that closeness and unanimity on that occasion, it was surely the last time such concord was known. And dealing with differences has occupied a primary place on the church's agenda ever since.

But Paul's prescription for dealing with diversity remains the most therapeutic means of healing the inevitable pain caused by the collision of contrasting opinions and practices.

First we must remember that however peculiar we may find the beliefs or acts of some Christians, they are in the church because God welcomed them! Dare we lift the bar of membership higher than God has? And God welcomed them warts and all, just as, in our more reflective moments, we must understand was the same magnanimous manner in which God received us.

Furthermore, each of us has been called to serve Christ where we are, with what we have, and according to understandings given to us. And we must allow others the same freedom we claim for ourselves.

The most helpful way of dealing with diversity, however, is the simple remembrance that we must always keep Christ at the center of our vision and our attention. It is when we take our eyes off our Lord and focus them on the faults of our sisters and brothers that we begin to lose the perspective with which we are called to view others. We are not required to see others through rose-colored glasses, but we are called upon to see others through the perspective of the love of Christ.

In past generations, there was a commonly quoted phrase that Christians frequently used to silence cruel judgments of others. Whatever the sins or weaknesses of the one being spoken of, someone in the group was likely to say, "But remember, he is someone for whom Christ died." And so is everyone you know, however difficult it may be for you to appreciate his or her peculiarities.

DAY 43
Read Romans 15

___

The teacher of a Sunday school class of small children had carefully related Jesus' story of the good Samaritan. Her young charges listened attentively as she told of the victim of the robbers lying wounded beside the road, and the priest and Levite who passed the injured man without offering assistance, and finally the good Samaritan who stopped and mercifully rendered the needed help. "Now," the teacher asked the children, "what did you learn from this story?" One eager young lad supplied the answer: "I learned that whenever I get into trouble, someone should help me out!"

Unfortunately, many people always think of themselves as the needy, the hurting, and those mistreated by life's circumstances. We take a kind of perverse delight in thinking of ourselves as poor, as the deserving recipients of the munificence of others. So when we hear Paul's words, "We who are strong ought to put up with the failings of the weak, and not to please ourselves," we are inclined to understand them as our claim on the tolerance and generosity of those more blessed than we are!

But Paul clearly intended his words to include every Christian— then and now. We are the strong, the rich, the blessed, from whom God expects a certain noblesse oblige. And since God's grace has made us strong, we owe to those less gifted the patience, tolerance, and understanding that Christ clearly offered us before his grace made us worthy recipients of such favors. Earlier in this epistle Paul wrote, "God proves his love for us in that while we still were sinners Christ died for us" (Romans 5:8). What magnanimity! What faith was demonstrated in that extravagant act, given to us even before we could begin to understand or appreciate it. That's how Christ welcomed us into the kingdom.

Think, then, of what is expected of us when we are enjoined to "welcome one another, therefore, just as Christ has welcomed you" (v. 7). Can any of us really live up to that supreme standard of forgiving love and acceptance? Perhaps not. But we are not excused from doing our best in that regard.

What if that standard were reversed, and Christ would welcome you and accept you by the same measurement of your welcome and acceptance of others? Remember that in our frequent praying of the Lord's Prayer, that is exactly what we ask for: "Forgive us our debts, as we forgive our debtors." Would we be content to pray, "Welcome us in exactly the same degree of understanding that we have shown in our acceptance of others"?

DAY 44

The last chapter of Paul's letter to the Romans presents many intriguing mysteries. It is a very personal postscript to what had been a mostly academic and transcendental treatise. There are twenty-four individuals mentioned in this closing chapter. Such a mention of individuals was a common practice of Paul's, especially when he was writing to churches where his own personal experience had brought him into relationships with the people whom he remembered in his writing.

But let us not forget that Paul had never yet been to Rome. How, then, had he forged these friendships with those whom he mentions with such affectionate regard? We know how those relationships began in the case of some of those named. Aquila and Priscilla had been residents of Rome before all Jews had been banished from that city. In their exile they came to Corinth, where Paul had recently established the church. They shared the tent-making trade with Paul, and it may have been that common link that brought them together, but soon they shared the Christian faith, as well.

From the scant information contained in each of Paul's laudatory listings, it is clear that somewhere along the way Paul's path had briefly merged with theirs, and their shared faith had encouraged a permanent friendship.

One wonders if Paul had any hint, along the way, that those with whom he shared a brief encounter would one day be part of the congregation that would provide for him comfort and support during his last imprisonment.

The ancient fable of Androcles and the Lion tells of a slave who once came upon a lion in agony. The animal had stepped on a thorn, and the thorn had pierced the flesh of his foot, making every step a painful ordeal. An angry lion is also a dangerous lion, but Androcles had compassion on the animal, and risked his own life to remove the thorn.

Many years later the slave was thrown into the Coliseum to face a lion and certain death. But the lion remembered the slave who had befriended him, and Androcles' life was spared.

You may meet many people today. Some of them will be pleasant, some will be unpleasant. But every one of them is a potential friend. And when you see them again, at some distant time and place on the road of life, will they be your friends or your enemies?

DAY 45
Read 1 Corinthians 1

We can only guess what prompted Paul to say some of the things he wrote to his correspondents. But lacking any certain knowledge in this regard, we may find it helpful to imagine a scenario in which Paul's words were tailor-made to fit the situation.

What situation, for example, might have prompted Paul to write at length about the Jews' and the Greeks' ridicule of Paul's preaching about Christ and the cross? Let us remember that Corinth was probably the most cosmopolitan city in the world at that time. In the eighteen months that Paul had labored there, he had spent endless hours in the *agora* (marketplace) debating with philosophers and teachers representing a broad scope of philosophical schools of thought. He was a skillful debater, and his broad background equipped him to converse intelligently with Jews, Romans, Greeks, and many others.

But Paul had left the fledgling church when he continued his missionary journeys. Perhaps Paul worried that the young Christians in that worldly metropolis would not be able to withstand the practiced verbal assaults of the perennial enemies of the church. So Paul, as he wrote this letter, recalled the classic arguments that the Jews and Greeks hurled at him.

First, the Jews found the story of Christ and the cross a stumbling block, because their concept of God could not accommodate any picture of God suffering or dying, especially in so shameful a manner as crucifixion. As a matter of fact, their own law had said (in Deuteronomy 21:22–23) that one who is hanged on a tree is accursed by God.

Furthermore, the Greeks argued that God is totally beyond the reach of human emotions, for if God were to feel sorrow or anger or joy, that would mean that in that moment, at least, God was moved and affected by a human being, in which case God would be dependent upon a human being.

But rather than resolutely denying such charges, Paul gladly adopts them and turns them into a statement of the most glorious attributes we can know about God. You are right, Paul said to the Jews and Greeks (and to the Corinthian Christians who would have to answer their denunciations in the marketplace), the crude story of the Christ of God, suffering, bleeding, and dying on the cross, is a glorious stumbling-block; a magnificent folly, for through such ugliness and sorrow, salvation is born!

DAY 46
Read 1 Corinthians 2

There is a very old story about a tribal chieftain named Caligula who owned some land along the southern edge of the vast realm ruled by the king named Cyrus, who made war against Caligula's meager forces and quickly defeated them.

Caligula and his wife were brought to stand before the king to receive their judgment, which ordinarily would have been an automatic death sentence. But Cyrus was impressed with Caligula as he stood before him, tall, strong and courageous. So Cyrus questioned him:

"Caligula," he asked, "what would you do if I were to spare your life?"

"I would be very grateful, sire," said Caligula, "and serve you always."

"And what would you do if I were to spare your wife?" the king asked.

"Sire," said Caligula, "if you would do that I would gladly give my life for you."

So impressed was Cyrus that he required of Caligula only an oath of allegiance and sent him home a free man.

Later, Caligula and his wife were at home discussing the day they were in the palace.

"Did you see the beautiful marble in the walls of the palace?" asked Caligula.

"No," she replied, "I didn't see it."

"Did you notice the tapestries on the walls of the palace?" Caligula asked.

"No," she replied, "I didn't see them."

"Well, surely," he said, "you saw that the king's throne was made of pure gold?"

"No," she replied, "I didn't see it."

"Then what did you see the day we stood before the king?" asked Caligula.

His wife replied, "I saw only the face of one who said he would die for me."

Marble, tapestries and gold—they all faded away. Controversies, differences of opinion, hurt feelings, they all lose their importance when we look upon the face of one who said he would die for us—and did.

So Paul said, "I decided to know nothing among you but Jesus Christ, and him crucified" (v. 2). And nothing else mattered!

Every Christian is a unique creation of God. It was God who, through Christ, called us to a new life. It must be acknowledged, however, that the production of each Christian is a collaborative effort. Unlike Topsy, we did not "jes' grow." Many hands supplied the effort and many hearts provided the caring that, together, made us what we are.

Paul's figure of the growth of a plant is an apt one: someone plants, someone else does the watering, another person provides the hard labor of cultivating, and yet another may do the harvesting. And while all play an essential part in the total process, none could have accomplished the miracle of growth, which is a secret only God knows.

But though the contribution of each would be futile without the miracle only God gives, it is proper for us to acknowledge, with gratitude, the contributions many others have made to our Christian identity. While every person would have his or her own list of contributors, let us not forget:

The teacher of our kindergarten class who first told us that God loves us.

The minister who knelt down to our level and looked, with a smile, into our faces, to show that we were precious to God and to God's representatives.

The parents or grandparents who saw that we faithfully attended Sunday school, even when we didn't particularly want to.

The composers and poets who created the hymns that put the profundities of the Christian faith within the reach of our participation.

The missionaries who were courageous enough and visionary enough to take the gospel of Christ into a foreign land—even when that "foreign land" was ours.

The translators who faced persecution and martyrdom to give us a Bible in a language we could read and understand.

People whose physical, spiritual, or emotional needs evoke from us the response that makes us instruments of divine grace.

So many people made it possible for God's miracle of growth to occur in your life. Doesn't that fact call for frequent and fervent prayers of gratitude?

"What do you have that you did not receive?" Paul asked the Corinthians, thereby laying groundwork for his theology of stewardship. It is not hyperbole, but demonstrable fact. We are given temporary use of the gifts God drops into our waiting laps, but we have in no sense earned or deserved them. They are gifts.

"But it's mine!" we say of our house, or our car, or some other possession that gives us pride of ownership. "I worked hard for years to earn it!" But ask yourself: Who gave you those years? Who gave you the strength and the ability to work? It was God who gave you those currencies. And if you take some of those currencies that God gave you, and use them to purchase something you want, doesn't it mean, in the final analysis, that it was God who gave you those things?

Jesus said, in his Sermon on the Mount, "Do not worry, saying 'What will we eat?' or 'What will we drink?' or 'What will we wear?' For it is the Gentiles who strive for all these things; and indeed your heavenly Father knows that you need all these things. But strive first for the kingdom of God and his righteousness, and all these things will be given to you as well" (Matthew 6:31–33). So the farmer (who depends upon the providential care of God, whether he realizes it or not) drops a seed into the ground and trusts the universe to give him what he needs. And, through a process so complex we could not understand it if we tried, the universe answers back with a harvest: bread, orange juice, or cotton, for us to eat or drink or wear.

> Back of the loaf is the snowy flour,
> Back of the flour the mill,
> Back of the mill is the sun and the showers,
> And the seed and the Father's will.
>
> –Maltie Babcock

What do you have that you have not received?

All our wealth (and despite our self-effacing modesty, we are among the world's most gifted people) is, therefore, an evidence of God's faith in us. God believes that we will use wisely and compassionately the vast resources that have been put into our hands. "It is required of stewards that they be found trustworthy," Paul reminded the Corinthians. And the more we have been given, the greater our responsibility.

What God has given us is a sign of God's grace. What we give back to God is evidence of our gratitude for that grace.

DAY 49
Read 1 Corinthians 5

It is important for us to remember that the Christians in Corinth were like a small island of piety in the midst of a sea of blasphemy. Corinth was well known as a city without rules and bereft of morals. Not only did the old pagan religions condone immorality, they incorporated it into their rituals. The Christians must have been as conspicuous in their chastity as a lone star against a black sky. Without doubt their lifestyle, which eschewed the hedonism for which Corinth was well known, drew both the ridicule and the denunciation of those who were content to stay in their sin.

Being a Christian in Corinth and living a life called for by that faith couldn't have been easy. There must have been a daily battle waged by the ungodly against the godly, and occasionally the ungodly scored a victory. We are informed of one such tragedy, in which a member of the church in Corinth forsook his faith to live a life of immoral abandon. How should the church deal with such a matter? It was important for Paul—and for the Corinthian Christians—to recognize that there are definite moral perimeters within which a Christian must live. And as compassionate as the Christian community must be in dealing with one who has failed to stay within those boundaries of decency, the standards must remain inviolate.

Forgiveness may restore a sinner to Christian fellowship, but sin is still sin, and its evil effects cannot be lightly dismissed. No matter how many times the laws of God may be transgressed, they remain in force.

But while the Christian community must be clear and consistent in its opposition to everything that is offensive to God's Holy Spirit within us, we must always seek to restore those who have sinned. We cannot do that by pretending that they have not sinned, or by accepting their immoral behavior without questioning it. A sick person cannot be healed by pretending that his illness does not exist, but by diagnosing the cause of the problem and offering a therapeutic remedy.

However, even while taking this high moral ground, we must always remember that none of us is entirely free of guilt. There have been times when we have transgressed the moral law of God. So it is in an attitude of humility that we seek to correct without condemning, so that, as Paul said of the sinner in the Corinthian church, "His spirit might be saved in the day of the Lord."

DAY 50

One fine day in June, many years ago, I stood nervously beside a beautiful young bride, and in reply to the sonorous questions put to me by the minister in front of me, I gave myself in marriage to that young lady. And in all the intervening years, and even to this very day, she held my life in her keeping. Though she has permitted me a certain amount of latitude in life, belonging to her has provided the framework within which my life has been lived. She does not establish rules for my conduct; nevertheless, I cannot do anything that I cannot do as a loving and faithful husband. Her love has made me free to be what I could never have been without her companionship and encouragement. Belonging to her has not made me a slave, but has given me the liberty to be my real self.

(I suspect that if asked, that young bride of so many years ago would affirm that in the same manner her life has been in my care and keeping.)

So Paul shows us how our relationship with Christ is more than acquaintance with a person of esteem, more than friendship with a cherished companion. Being a Christian is more like giving ourselves—totally and joyfully—into the keeping of Jesus Christ in a spiritual covenant not entirely unlike the bond of marriage. Such an act does not diminish our lives, but enriches them beyond measure. "You are not your own," Paul says. "For you were bought with a price" (vv. 19b, 20).

So Paul is able to say (almost boastfully, so great is his gratitude for this grace) that "all things are lawful for me" (v. 12). That is, he is not bound by any laws! How nice, not to have to worry about breaking any law, no matter what you do! But the reason Paul is able to say that is that he is bound by a higher authority than law: it is the authority of love.

On the statute books of every state there are many laws defining how marriage partners must behave toward each other, under pain of punishment. If a prospective bride and groom undertook to study all such laws in the state of their residence before proceeding with the marriage, they might never get around to tying the knot.

But there is an easier and surer way to fulfill all those laws: love one another.

So Augustine was right: living the Christian life is not a matter of scrupulously obeying laws, but of giving oneself in loving commitment to the Lord of Life. And in that confinement is liberty indeed.

DAY 51
Read 1 Corinthians 7

An old caveat is helpful in considering Paul's teachings about women: "To know all is to understand all; to understand all is to forgive all." For it cannot be denied that Paul's view of marriage is less than felicitous, and his general attitude toward women appears to be less charitable than Paul elsewhere urges us to be toward all people. What, then, is there about Paul that we need to know to understand about his negative attitude toward women?

The first thing we must know is that Paul had almost certainly been married at one time. There are two facts that support such a contention. In the first place, the Jewish law set forth that one of the basic qualifications for a Rabbi was that he must be at least thirty years old, and married. Paul was a Rabbi, and frequently claimed that he had not failed the Jewish law in any respect. This one fact alone would almost certainly prove that Paul had at one time been married.

But if it is clear that Paul had been married at one time, it is equally clear that at the time of his writing of this letter, he was no longer married, for he said, "To the unmarried and the widows I say that it is well for them to remain unmarried as I am." What happened, then, to Paul's former marriage? Bible scholars offer two possible explanations:

Perhaps Paul's wife died at some earlier time, ending a tender relationship between young sweethearts, who had looked forward to many years together. Imagine the grief and shock to Paul, if that had been the case. It would not be too difficult to picture him channeling his energies and passions into his magnificent obsession—the church of Jesus Christ. Many a man—and many a woman—has turned a painful loss into a redeeming crusade. If love had come to mean sorrow to Paul, it is possible he may have wished his friends to avoid such pain.

Or perhaps Paul's dramatic conversion to the Christian faith alienated him from his wife, if she did not share his new faith. (And one can easily understand Paul's warning to Christians not to be yoked with unbelievers.)

But in either case, let us be understanding of the pain and loss that may have skewed Paul's thinking on this subject. And if he was wrong in this matter (and in another passage Paul admits that such was possible in his views on this subject), let us forgive him, as we must ask forgiveness for our mistakes that have resulted from our pains and troubles. As the Native American proverb said it, "Do not judge another until you have walked a mile in his moccasins."

DAY 52
Read 1 Corinthians 8

In the numerous pagan temples for which Corinth was well known, the usual form of worship was the offering of sacrifices. As in the worship in the Jewish temple, these sacrifices took the form of living creatures–sheep, oxen, and others. Sacrifices were offered every day in Corinth's pagan temples, and on holy days the animals would have numbered in the thousands.

The obvious solution to the problem of all these animal carcasses piling up was to butcher the remains and sell the meat in markets. With this constant supply of clean animals made available for commercial sale, it is unlikely that any meat had to be imported. The Corinthians simply patronized one of the temple markets.

But apparently some members of the early church had found fault with this practice. The implication of Paul's treatment of this subject suggests that he did not share their antipathy. How could a pagan god or goddess contaminate meat offered as sacrifices, since pagan deities were figments of the imagination of their devotees, and therefore did not exist? One suspects that such picky quibbling might secretly have repulsed Paul. Far too much time, thought, and passion are expended on matters of minor concern, when there are gigantic issues that should engage the Christian's mind.

Nevertheless, Paul dealt with the matter with utter magnanimity. "If my eating [this pagan temple] meat causes anyone to stumble, I will gladly forego the meat." Paul's remarkably concise and lucid solution to the problem underscores three important facts:

First, we must always remember that people are different in every way, and just because we see things in a certain way is no proof that others will see them in the same way. What may be a matter of infinitesimal concern to us may present infinitely difficult problems to someone else.

Second, there are some matters in which logic and reason are the wrong approaches to a human problem. Whether one is right or wrong, one is still a human being, loved by God, and it is in that attitude that we must seek to understand.

Finally, there are social consequences to all our acts, and whether or not something is right and good in itself is less to be considered than what our participation in that something will do to others. It may be a difficult and costly discipline, as Jesus himself discovered on Calvary, but we are our brothers' and our sisters' keeper. And we will be held responsible not only for what we have done, but for what they have done because of how our actions have influenced them. May God have mercy on our souls!

From the vantage point of our time and place, it seems both lamentable and unnecessary that Paul should have to expend so much of his time and energy defending his own claim to apostleship. Other than Jesus himself, no other figure towers so imposingly in the earliest history of the church. While some may claim that Paul's prominence in early church history was enhanced by the fact that Dr. Luke meticulously reported his words and work, still his contributions stand alone as evidence of the magnificent contributions of an extraordinary leader. Nevertheless, to paraphrase the words of Jesus, "Prophets are not without honor, except in their hometown"...and in their own time (Mark 6:4, altered).

So everywhere Paul went he had to justify his own claim to apostleship, and he always began that apologetic by reporting that he had been an eyewitness of the Risen Christ, for such had been the case in that dramatic encounter on the Road to Damascus.

But Paul had further evidence to point to, in his effort to establish the legitimacy of his claim of apostleship. Speaking boldly to the Christians at Corinth he said, "You are the seal of my apostleship" (v. 2).

In those days important documents that had to be delivered by messenger were secured with sealing wax. Before the wax cooled completely, the writer imprinted his distinctive signet or crest into it. When the document was delivered, it was that seal that proved the authenticity of the paper and the identity of the writer. So Paul said that the Corinthians were the seal that established the genuineness of his claim to apostleship.

The proof of the expertise of an elementary school teacher may be found in the number of people who know how to read and write because of her instruction. No document framed and hung on the wall can testify to her excellence as a teacher if there are not those people whose education proves her abilities.

Likewise a doctor's reputation is not established by his academic credentials, but by those people whose lives have been spared because of his dedicated ministries.

What evidence, then, is there that you are a follower of Christ? Are there those people who are Christians because of your example or witness or compassion, and who would, therefore, be the seal of the genuineness of your claim as a Christian?

DAY 54
Read 1 Corinthians 10

A young man had been caught in an act of mischief and was being scolded by his father. The youth tearfully defended himself, "But it wasn't my fault. I got sucked in by circumstances!" Such has been the ubiquitous claim of people who have fallen victim to temptation ever since the Garden of Eden. In his treatment of this painful subject, Paul makes some important points worth pondering:

First, we are never immune to temptation. Being baptized Christians does not protect us from the power of sin's seduction, any more than Jesus was sheltered from its enticements. And even when he had soundly defeated the tempter in the wilderness, the scripture reports that the devil "departed from him until an opportune time" (Luke 4:13). Whether we are wise enough to be always watching for occasions when we might succumb to temptation, we must be aware that the tempter is.

The second weapon in the armory of defense against temptation is the remembrance that you do not face your trial alone. There is no temptation that you can face that has not been faced successfully by others. The battleground where we are confronted by temptation is littered with both the stars and the scars left by those who have fought this same battle ahead of us, and each of us decides which of those souvenirs we will take from that conflict. And if our choice is not a deliberately chosen star, it will be an inescapable scar left on our soul.

There is always a moment, however fleeting, when you—and you alone—decide the outcome of the battle in which you are engaged.

Finally, Paul assures us that we are never left without some escape as we struggle with temptation. "God is faithful," Paul reminds us, "and he will not let you be tested beyond your strength, but with the testing he will also provide the way out so that you may be able to endure it" (v. 13).

A small girl whose parents could not find a way to break her habit of sucking her thumb finally asked her one day why she did it. She thought a moment and replied, "I guess it's because I want to so good."

And that is, of course, the reason we do things that are wrong for us: because we want to so good. So the remedy for temptation is to find something (or someone) that means more to us than the act that tempts us. And in Paul's case, that supreme attraction was to Christ. If pleasing Christ is uppermost in our minds and hearts, no lesser charm can lead us astray.

DAY 55
Read 1 Corinthians 11

In various parts of the country it is called by a variety of names: pot-luck supper, pitch-in dinner, basket lunch, covered dish supper. But the principle is always the same. Each person or family brings what it has or can afford to acquire, and all the food is spread out on a serving table, and every participant chooses freely from the combined fare. Although it sounds like a modern means of stimulating fellowship, it is one of the authentic souvenirs of the early church. In Paul's day it was called the agape feast or love feast. And when properly conducted it was a token of the love Jesus said would be the distinguishing characteristic of his disciples.

Let us remember that the early church was an authentic melting pot of humanity. There were Jews and Greeks, slaves and free, male and female, highly educated and unlearned, rich and poor. It is altogether likely that the church was the only place where they could gather as equals. What a beautiful opportunity it must have been for people who were ordinarily segregated from each other because of cultural or economic differences to come together as brothers and sisters in one family.

The sharing of food was a token of this fellowship. Without doubt there would be some at the agape feast who looked forward all week to that smorgasbord, because their resources allowed only a meager fare at home. And there were those for whom a sumptuous meal was a daily occurrence. What a delightful experience that both kinds of people could come together and receive what each needed most: food for the hungry, and an experience of sharing for the affluent.

But a tragic short-circuiting of this tradition had taken place. The affluent stayed in their insular coterie of the well-to-do, eating the prime rib and caviar they had brought, while the poor members were left with only the gruel and rice they had brought. And when, in the midst of this feast, the Lord's supper was celebrated, the compassionate Christ was dishonored instead of honored.

Both the rich and the poor members suffered from this tragedy, for both left the experience still lacking what they had come needing: food for the poor, and the opportunity to experience sharing love for the rich.

What we take home from the table may depend, at least in some measure, upon what we bring to it.

A little girl was watching her mother make jelly. The mother poured the colored liquid into a variety of vessels—some tall and slender, some short and broad, some ornate and others plain. In amazement at this simple process the girl exclaimed, "Oh, mother, isn't it wonderful? It fits them all!"

So the grace of God exactly fits our need, regardless of how our lives and circumstances may differ from others. A surprising but authentic corollary of this is the fact that each of us—however dissimilar we may be to others—has a unique contribution to make to the kingdom of God. And what we have to give, by some strange but wonderful miracle of grace, just happens to be exactly what the realm of heaven needs.

When God calls us to holy service, we bring with us the gifts and graces we have been given, remembering that it was the Lord who gave us those gifts in the first place, and matched them with some need that God will show us. And if the work of God in this world seems to limp along ineffectually at times, we must see that tragedy as evidence that someone isn't using his or her gifts as the Giver intended.

Paul's beautiful visual parable of the church being like a body with many parts would be difficult to improve upon. And most of us have had firsthand experience with the pain and difficulty we suffer when even a minute part of our bodies isn't behaving as it should. Think of the suffering we endure over one aching tooth or a corn on one toe!

Perhaps an equally adept illustration could be found in a modern automobile, which has thousands of parts, many of them quite small. But think of the trouble that results when a fuse—no larger than a medicine capsule—fails, or a screw holding an essential part of the engine works loose and falls out.

The part you play in the church, and in God's kingdom, may seem very small and inconsequential to you. But without the part that you alone can play, some indispensable quality will be missing, or some needed human service may be neglected, or some vital connection with God may be jeopardized.

A sign on the wall of a business office warned: "Keep Busy! The Boss Is Watching to See if He Could Do Without You!" God has given you something that is meant to provide an essential service to the world and its Maker. And God is watching to see if you are providing that necessary service that only you can provide.

It is an indisputable fact of nature that often something beautiful emerges from circumstances that are ugly and painful, like the labor pains that produce a radiant new life.

So the thirteenth chapter of First Corinthians is unquestionably one of the most sublime utterances in all holy writ. But this beautiful celebration of the most magnificent quality of which human beings are capable was evoked by a bitter quarrel in the church. And this internecine strife was provoked by a disagreement over what constituted proper worship.

There were those who had found an exciting and enthusiastic experience in speaking in tongues. They had observed their pagan neighbors indulging in this release of their emotions in the ecstatic speech that said nothing lucid, but felt good to the speaker.

On the other hand, there were those who preferred a more rational approach to their religious experience. They were embarrassed by the crudeness of the tongue speakers, but they found great satisfaction in writing creeds and liturgical materials, and debating the truths upon which their faith was built.

There were others in the church who found God in the experience of prayer. It was on their knees that God became real to them, and they didn't understand how anyone could possibly be Christian without their prayer disciplines.

Finally, there were members of the church who clucked their tongues over the raucous tongue speaking, and they couldn't stay awake to study theology, and their knees hurt when they knelt to pray. But they loved their Lord, and proved it by rolling up their sleeves and tackling projects that glorified God and served the needy.

And while Paul does not dismiss any discipline of worship, he does say to those whose belief that their way of worship was the only legitimate way, "I will show you a...more excellent way" (1 Corinthians 12:31). And that more excellent way is love.

I suspect that when we come to the end of our way, we will not count among our treasures the memory of any enthusiasm in any form of worship, or any expertise in theology, or any groundbreaking pilgrimages in prayer, or any monumental contributions of sacrifice or generosity. Rather, I suspect the treasures we will count as among our greatest riches will be those we have purchased by the giving of our love.

DAY 58
Read 1 Corinthians 14

While it is true that the early church had some gifted and highly proficient professional leaders (such as Paul and the living apostles and a few others), it is also true that most Christian congregations had no such leadership. Nor was there a rich tradition of worship materials for local churches to draw upon. It was a kind of "do-it-yourself" church, in which the worship experiences lacked the polish and order we have come to expect from our churches.

Paul's practical advice to the Corinthian church regarding the conduct of worship intimates that even with the kind of disciplined leadership that Paul and Apollos had given the church, the members of that church still depended upon the inspiration of the moment to provide for the spiritual needs of the people.

Despite the obvious shortcomings of such a casual attitude toward worship, one sometimes wonders if the church did not make a mistake when it eventually decided to leave the conduct of worship to a professional clergy. In many churches today the congregants want nothing more than to sit back and allow their pastor to worship on their behalf. But the very word "liturgy," which refers to the prescribed ritual for public worship, comes from the Greek words *laos* (people) and *ergon* (work). Thus, worship is the work of the people. It is what we do as Christians.

While not every Christian is fluent in speech or poised in public leadership, every disciple of Christ must find some venue and some experience in which to express his or her faith and thanksgiving and praise to God in his or her own way.

It is lamentable that few homes—even among Christians—have grace before meals at the family table or frequent devotional experiences at home. It was in those tiny congregations that many a man or woman—and many a boy or girl—learned to pray and lead others in worship.

To make a start in restoring the work of worship to the people, let us encourage people at worship not just to listen to the pastor's prayer, but to pray as he leads, and praise God as the choir sings its praises. When a Christian goes to church, it should be an experience of Christian growth and giving—not just of rest and receiving.

DAY 59
Read 1 Corinthians 15

Paul was never timid or ambiguous in his proclamation of the central miracle upon which the gospel rests: the resurrection of Christ from the dead. It was no once-a-year season's greeting but the validating evidence of the Lordship of Jesus Christ. Upon the strength of that astonishing event Paul based his theology, his ministry, his faith, and his life. "If there is no resurrection of the dead," Paul proclaimed, "then Christ has not been raised; and if Christ has not been raised, then our proclamation has been in vain and your faith has been in vain" (vv. 13–14).

The resurrection—both Christ's and ours—is not a matter to be understood biologically, but theologically. Sifting through the ashes of an ancient event just outside the city walls of Jerusalem two millennia ago will not yield the key to our quest. Nor can logic build a case that will make that magnificent event tenable to the cautious cynic. The resurrection is not so much to be discovered in the test tubes of our intelligence as to be celebrated in the lyrical excesses of an ecstatic discovery. It is not in the scientific textbooks that we find the literature that proves the resurrection, but in the housetop shoutings of those who have discovered that there are some things too good not to be true. It is the final, undeniable verdict within our human experience that God is true, and will always be true.

And where did Paul find the evidence that convinced him of the unarguable truth of the resurrection? It was in his own experience. He had been a persecutor of Christians, an avowed enemy of the church, a bigot and a hater "breathing threats and murder" against the followers of Christ. But in his meeting with the real presence of the resurrected Christ on the Road to Damascus, he became a new man, a man resurrected from the sin and hate and hopelessness of his former life, to a new life that marched to the drumbeat of God's promises and celebrated in a daily discovery of Christ's dependable presence.

And this is how the resurrection is always proved: not in someone else's life, but in our own. And when death confronts us at the end of our road of life, the wide open door to a glorious eternity will prove to us at last the truth that must be experienced to be understood: that with the Creator of life, life goes on.

If you believe in the resurrection, it is because it has happened to you.

In nearly every reference Paul made in his writings to the resurrection, he followed it with a "therefore." As a result of our belief in Christ's new life, and the new life we have received from him, there should be a logical consequence in some practical action. Paul's conclusion to his long treatise on the resurrection in the fifteenth chapter is: "Therefore, my beloved, be steadfast, immovable, always excelling in the work of the Lord, because you know that in the Lord your labor is not in vain."

Then the apostle begins the next chapter by continuing that thought. (And let us remember that there were no chapter divisions in Paul's original manuscript, but that these were added centuries later.) "Always excelling in the work of the Lord" was the logical consequence of living in the light that shined out of the empty tomb. No miserly or cautious response to those in need would give evidence of the heart-expanding experience of the new life in Christ. But the brass-tacks translation of that new magnanimity is found in Paul's exhortation to give a generous offering for the relief of the Christian brothers and sisters in Jerusalem who were being subjected to deprivations and persecutions because of their faith.

Paul's instruction to the Corinthian Christians was the same as he had given to Christians elsewhere: "On the first day of every week" (that is, regularly, and as a part of the worship experienced in the church), "each of you" (no one is excused in the giving of gifts to God, for God has given something to everyone) "is to put aside" (gifts to God should come first from our income, and kept separate from the rest of our resources, for they are God's) "and save" (what we give to God we do not give away, but lay up for ourselves in heaven) "whatever extra you earn" (it is not what we need for ourselves and our families that God wants us to give, but what we have left beyond our basic needs).

Aside from this splendid message on Christian stewardship, Paul reminded the Corinthian Christians that they were members not just of a congregation, but of a church. And it was a church whose membership extended far beyond their hometown and included many whom they had never met, but who were members of the Body of Christ, and , therefore, their brothers and sisters.

In the magnanimity of our response to the needs of our brothers and sisters around the world we demonstrate the resurrection in our lives.

Consolation seems such a second-rate quality, as we ordinarily use that word. "It's a pity you didn't win the grand prize," the unctuous television quizmaster says, "but we have a consolation prize for you." And that consolation prize turns out to be a month's supply of the washday detergent that sponsors the quiz show. Or, "It's a shame you didn't win the election," we tell the dejected candidate, "but if it's any consolation, you got a full three and a half percent of the vote." Small comfort indeed!

But despite the warped implications that have come to be associated with it, consolation is a grand word, and the divine gift it signifies is one of the highest expressions of God's concern for us.

Picture Simeon, the aged holy man who loved God and cherished the nation whose God was the Lord. In his length of years he had watched his beloved Israel suffer the indignities of being enslaved to a pagan power. He had watched the sacred traditions trampled under the feet of Gentile invaders. He had heard the mournful wailing of the prophets, "How long, O Lord, how long?" But still he hoped for the redemption of his people, and a resurrection of their national supremacy. Still he prayed that the right would be vindicated.

So day by day he went to the temple to pray. And for what did he pray? The scripture says it plainly, "for the consolation of Israel." What? That weak old quality of consolation? Surely he could pray for something more substantial and more practical than consolation. But when he saw the infant Christ, whose parents brought him into the temple for blessing, Simeon knew that his prayer for the consolation of Israel had at last been answered! Christ was the comfort, the strength, the redemption, the hope and the joy of Israel.

Consolation is an omnibus blessing, which only an omnibus God can grant.

So in writing to the Corinthian Christians, Paul knew that their hurts were many and painful; their disappointments were disheartening; their needs were pauperizing. So Paul lifted up their hearts to receive the gift of God that fits every need. And it could be expressed only in the word that Paul used nine times in four verses: consolation!

Listen, child of God: Whatever your need, whatever your hurt, whatever your sorrow, there is a God of all consolation who is uniquely able to give you everything you need.

DAY 62

Scientific research has demonstrated that what we smell has a greater power to evoke memories than what we see or hear. Most of us have happy memories that are brought to the surface again when we catch a breath of a long-remembered fragrance.

Perhaps it is the aroma of a freshly baked apple pie, just removed from the oven; or maybe it is the scent of honeysuckle in the evening, or the unmistakable smell of the interior of a new car, or a certain perfume that mother always wore.

Such fragrances provide a powerful attraction. Indeed, botanists tell us that the lovely scent produced by many flowers has the primary purpose of attracting the bees and other insects that pay for their small draft of nectar by accomplishing the necessary task of pollination.

And no one can doubt that a bakery's most effective advertisement is the redolence of freshly baked bread that reaches out from the oven to seize passersby by the nose, to pull them into the bakery to buy.

Think, then, what an enormous responsibility Paul laid upon the Corinthian Christians (and upon himself—and us!) when he said, "We are the aroma of Christ to God among those who are being saved and among those who are perishing" (v. 15). Paul expressed the same thought a bit farther into this letter by saying, "We are ambassadors for Christ, since God is making his appeal through us" (5:20). Both an aroma and an ambassador have two primary purposes: first, to be an accurate representative of the entity being represented, and, second, to reach out to those who need to be made aware of the entity being personified.

So as the aroma (or ambassador) of Christ, we must first seek to become as much like Christ as it is humanly possible (with God's help) to be; then we must seek to make Christ known to those who do not know him. And our greatest witness will probably not be the words we speak, but rather the marks of Christ's presence that are clearly shown in our lives.

If there is anyone who knows you but does not know Christ, you are not doing your job as the aroma of Christ!

DAY 63

In Paul's day very few people were known beyond their own home country. Travel was both expensive and arduous, and provisions for hospitality to strangers were almost unheard of. If a traveler had a relative or friend (or even a friend of a friend) in the town of his destination, common courtesy would have given the traveler the right to expect food and lodging from such a source, even at the cost of inconvenience or sacrifice on the part of the host.

But lacking such personal contacts, the sojourner had to rely upon letters of recommendation, written by those who knew the traveler. In such a letter the writer offered his own character and resources as guarantee of the integrity of the traveler. If the writer was a person of importance, such a letter would open doors and secure the benefits needed by the traveler. With that kind of guarantee, one could venture far from home with confidence.

A similar service is rendered, in this age, by credit cards. We may venture far beyond our home precincts without worrying about our limited resources if we have in our pocket some evidence that someone has recommended us. The hotel desk clerk or the restaurant waiter may not know us, but if he knows American Express or Visa or Discover, he accepts their testimonial to our credit worthiness.

There are two ways of seeing this custom as a clue to one aspect of our Christian discipleship. First, when we put on the identity of Christ, we take the name of Jesus as our guarantee of acceptance. Wherever in the world the name of Jesus is known and revered, we may safely go, for those who know Christ will accept us as brother or sister. An old hymn says:

Take the name of Jesus with you, child of sorrow and of woe;
It will joy and comfort give you. Take it, then, where'er you go.

But this custom also implies an important responsibility in our life of Christian discipleship. As we take on Christ's name, so he takes on ours. We become his introduction into our world, and his recommendation to those who know us.

Wherever you go today, and whatever you do, remember that there will be those who will judge Christ and his church by what they see in you.

DAY 64
Read 2 Corinthians 4

A college professor suffered the death of his wife, his life partner for almost half a century. His colleagues watched in alarm as this once meticulous man began to appear slovenly in his dress and grooming. His apartment likewise began to take on the appearance of a slum. The wallpaper hung in weary festoons from crumbling walls. The curtains at the windows had surrendered all evidence of their original color.

In charitable concern for their fellow professor, some of his colleagues called upon him and expressed their dismay at the shabby countenance his life had assumed. The object of their concern looked around him at the unkempt house and at his own appearance in the cracked and dusty mirror on the wall. In astonishment he said, "I had no idea...it all happened so slowly."

And that is precisely how most of life's most dramatic changes occur—not suddenly, but gradually: day by day.

There is a stern warning here for people who may not realize how their daily conduct is projecting a future they would not want. No one ever sets out to become an alcoholic: it just happens, one little sip at a time. And no one ever intends to become selfish, or dishonest, or evil. Those destinies, too, are forged so slowly that we can hardly perceive that it is happening at all.

But equally amazing is the fact that glorious destinies are also achieved on a "day-by-day" basis. Even so magnificent a transformation as our metamorphosis from a creature of the Earth to an heir of God is a pilgrimage, which requires daily progress.

"Our inner nature is being renewed day by day" (v. 16), Paul said. That means one day at a time.

The Chinese coined a proverb that is unquestionably true in any language: "The journey of a million miles begins with a single step." And that is certainly true of the greatest journey of all: the odyssey of the soul from Earth to heaven. And if you do not take each day's step when it appears before you, you will be slipping farther and farther away from your goal.

It all happens "day by day."

DAY 65
Read 2 Corinthians 5

When Stephen Langton, thirteenth-century archbishop of Canterbury, devised the chapter and verse divisions of the Bible, he bequeathed to centuries of Bible readers a convenient method by which scriptural passages could be easily identified and located. Unfortunately–albeit unintentionally–he also interrupted the logical flow of some of the Bible's most majestic masterpieces of theological thought. A prime example of this misfortune may be observed in the last three verses of the fourth chapter of Second Corinthians and the first ten verses of the fifth chapter. Taken together (as they should always be) they give us one of the most triumphant and heartening pictures of the Christian concept of eternal life that the Bible has to offer.

The movement of thought takes us from the inevitable hopelessness of this world's realities (our outer nature, wasting away), through the transition of death (this slight momentary affliction), to the promised resurrection (clothed with our heavenly dwelling). This glorious logic must be seen together. Otherwise a Christian can make no sense of the "groaning in travail" that this life often resembles.

In seeking for a parable, Paul depicts a camper in a tent. The tent is small, cramped, and inconvenient, though it is a necessary shelter from the vicissitudes of wind, rain, and cold. But one day, tired of such confinement, the camper leaves his tent to discover that he is in a beautiful rainbowed valley under the canopy of a cloudless sky. What a glorious discovery. It is like being released from prison, or recovering from a debilitating illness. What a relief!

And it is that relief that Paul sets before us as the next chapter of life that lies just beyond the experience of death.

"So," Paul says, "we are always confident" (v. 6). It is the confidence of knowing how the last chapter of life will turn out. It is the confidence Jesus felt when on the cross he could say, "Father, into your hands I commend my spirit" (Luke 23:46). His enemies could take his body and subject it to the blood of pain and the muck of shame. But they could not touch his soul–his very life. For it was safe in the strong hands of a loving God.

With that assurance we can live confidently, too!

A bumper-sticker slogan puts it this way: "Christians are like tea bags. Their real strength comes out when they are in hot water." And Paul knew all about hot water!

Earlier, in his first letter to the Corinthians, Paul had recited a catalog of hurts and dangers he had suffered in his service to Christ. Now, a few years later (and, no doubt, more scarred from the continuing abuse) Paul offers an even longer tabulation of the vicissitudes that have befallen him in his pursuit of the mission Christ laid upon him.

But one gets the feeling that Paul's recitation is not a plea for pity, but rather a boast. Each hurt and injury and misfortune that he had endured with patience and determination had become a shining gem in the diadem of his victorious apostleship. But as Paul emphasized numerous times, his boast was not of his own strength, but of the strength provided by the spirit of Christ in him.

It should be remembered that Christians are not uniquely susceptible to troubles. As Job unerringly pointed out, "Human beings are born to trouble just as sparks fly upward" (Job 5:7). Both Job and Paul—and countless millions of other saints through the centuries—discovered that righteousness does not immunize us against tribulation. Jesus warned his disciples, "In the world you have tribulation" (John 16:33, RSV). He never said a truer word.

But the same thing may be said of evildoers. The way of the transgressor is hard, indeed. For every mafia boss who rides around in his chauffeur-driven limousine, there are a hundred petty crooks who do not know where their next meal is coming from. No matter which path you choose in life, you will be no stranger to trouble.

But in one thing Christians have a decided edge. We may not be able to avoid trouble altogether, but we know where to go—and whom to ask—to find the strength to endure, and to make those scars turn into stars. And with that dependable help, we may watch our stumbling blocks become stepping-stones. And perhaps one day we may look back upon our difficulties and realize that it was in those experiences that we learned how to trust God.

To grasp the depth of joy Paul felt at the return of Titus, as reported in this passage, we must remind ourselves of the circumstances that prompted Paul's letters, and the effect. Rather than the two letters that have been preserved for us in the New Testament canon, scholars believe Paul penned at least four epistles to that church. No other congregation evoked such strong passions from Paul. He grieved for the divisions and other difficulties that confronted that church. Many of those problems he addressed in the writing that we call First Corinthians. Apparently that letter stirred up such animosity among the Corinthian disciples that Paul felt it necessary to pay a visit to the church. But what he had hoped would be a fence-mending expedition failed to achieve that hoped-for resolution and had the tragic effect of stirring up even more rancor among the Corinthians.

One might say to Paul at this point, "Cheer up! Things could be worse!" And, sure enough, he cheered up, and things promptly got worse! He wrote the Corinthians another letter, which he surely intended to be a defense of his position, but which he feared–after he had posted the letter–that the Corinthians would see only as another severe condemnation. Paul dispatched the letter by way of a young follower named Titus. But Paul could hardly wait for the return of Titus to hear how the Corinthian Christians had received the letter, and whether the recipients of his letter were now impossibly and forever alienated from him, or whether it could be hoped that they accepted his letter in good grace, and restored him to their hearts.

How Paul must have agonized as he awaited the return of Titus. Finally, unable to endure the suspense a day longer, Paul left Troas and traced the road by which Titus would be returning to Troy. At some spot along the road they met. Paul scanned the face of Titus to catch any forewarning of his message. But what Paul saw gave him great consolation. Titus had brought good news indeed! The hostility was over. The Corinthians saw Paul's corrective exhortations as evidences of his pastoral love, and not as expressions of condemnation. No wonder Paul was overwhelmed by joy in the arrival of Titus, for Titus was good news wrapped up in a person, the means by which reconciliation had taken place, the mediator through which holy love and human frailty had met.

Such a person is always a magnificent blessing, whether that person is Titus, or Jesus Christ, or you!

DAY 68
Read 2 Corinthians 8

A small church found itself without the services of a custodian, and the pastor placed a "help-wanted" ad in the local newspaper, asking applicants for the position to come to the church the following morning to be interviewed. But when the minister arrived at the church the next morning, there was just one young man waiting to see him.

Sizing him up, the minister began, without any preliminary comments, to interview him. "Young man," he asked, "are you willing to get up early every morning, and work hard all day, and do all the hard and disagreeable tasks no one else wants to do?"

The young man paused a moment and blinked his eyes before replying, "Well, I guess so."

"And," the clergyman continued, "can you take orders and receive criticism without spouting back?" Again, the young man indicated, reluctantly, that he could.

"And," the minister said, "will you wash windows, scrub floors, mow the lawn, shovel show, and do all the other difficult tasks that may be assigned you?"

At this point the young man cut in to say, "Reverend, I came this morning to ask you to preside at the wedding for me and my fiancée. But if marriage involves all that, maybe I'd better think it over a little more."

But whether marriage involves precisely those onerous duties, it does require that we pledge to each other the all-encompassing love and commitment that may sometimes require the performance of such duties as we might ordinarily prefer to avoid. When we give ourselves to love and cherish another person—for better or worse, for richer or poorer, in sickness and in health—we are not ruling out any sacrifice, any demand. And when a loving husband or wife makes heroic sacrifices to care for an ailing spouse, it is merely the logical extension of the wedding-day promise that began "I will."

So while Paul was grateful and heartened by the generous gift the Macedonian Christians had given for the relief of the suffering saints in Jerusalem, he was not in the least surprised, for "they gave themselves first to the Lord" (v. 5).

And when you give yourself first to the Lord, no demand will be too exacting, no sacrifice too costly. The love of the Lord Jesus may not require our death, but it certainly requires our life.

Like many another Christian leader since Paul's time, the apostle sought to motivate his hearers to generosity in their giving to an important Christian cause by reminding them of the magnanimity demonstrated in the stewardship of others. In the previous chapter Paul proudly reported the generous gift given by the Macedonians. Now he reveals that in the same way he had reported to the Macedonians how greathearted the Corinthians were in the gift they planned to give!

Purists would object, I suppose, to this competitive motivation to stimulate giving. But it is well to note that when Paul reported the work or spirit of one congregation to another, it was always done to commend, not to disparage the church referred to. But Paul also recognized the importance of our Christian responsibility to provide for others an example. Even Jesus admonished us, "Let your light shine before others, so that they may see your good works and give glory to your Father in heaven" (Matthew 5:16). And Paul frequently enjoined his readers to "outdo one another" in various evidences of Christian conduct.

Paul also employed other motivations for generosity: being stingy closes our hearts so that we do not receive abundantly; God will love us if we give cheerfully; we may take pride in making many good works possible. On and on Paul employs the standard (if not quite theologically circumspect) stimuli for generosity in giving to the continuing work of Christ.

But Paul leaves for last the one cardinal reason for our generosity: "because of the surpassing grace of God that he has given you" (v. 14). In the face of that grace of God, which led God to give the indescribable gift of Jesus' life on the cross for our sakes, how can our response be anything less than the most gallant generosity of which our resources are capable? Indeed, anything less would be an insult to God.

As the hymn writer said it:

Love so amazing, so divine
Demands my soul, my life, my all!

True Christian stewardship is not about us, but about God.

DAY 70
Read 2 Corinthians 10

It is clear that Paul had been subjected to much mean-spirited criticism. Some people objected to his theology, others to the manner in which he expressed himself. The barrage of disparagement had even reached to the depths of deploring the apostle's physical appearance. And there is ample evidence to suggest that such criticisms—irrelevant as they might have been—were true. Though no description of Paul's appearance may be found in the New Testament, various other sources (like the second-century document called "The Acts of Thekla and Paul") report that he was small of stature, bent, bowlegged, bald, and had a hooked nose. It is not likely that he won many converts to Christ by his appearance!

Dealing with criticism is always difficult, especially when it is true! When we are subjected to false aspersions, we do, at least, have the truth on our side. But when the criticisms are true, we are left without defenses.

And although Paul's defensiveness shows between the lines of his reply, it is clear that his strategy was to claim that all such negative comments were beside the point. His message was not himself, but his Lord. And if any boasting was to be done, it would have to recognize that Christ was the source of all victories and achievements.

One of Aesop's lesser-known fables tells of a frog and a crow who had a wonderful arrangement for transporting the frog to the warm South for the winter. The frog persuaded the crow to tie a string around his foot. Then the frog put the other end of the string in his mouth, and enjoyed a free ride to the balmy climes. All proceeded as planned until another crow flew alongside the tandem fliers and exclaimed "My, what a clever idea. Who thought of it?" The frog could not ignore such an opportunity to claim the praise and opened his mouth to say, "I did!" And those were the last words spoken by that particular frog.

And many a good idea, and many a fine achievement have been defiled by someone's insistence upon receiving the credit. But however much we may contribute to the good works that are usually attributed to our effort, we must be honest enough to acknowledge that there is a Senior Partner whose resources and wisdom and efforts were invested long before we undertook our little projects.

If anyone boasts, let him boast in the Lord.

Reading Paul's letters is like listening to one side of a telephone conversation. What we hear may be lucid and helpful in itself, but how much more it might mean to us if we knew what circumstances or words evoked Paul's written witness, and what may have resulted from it. At least we may read between the lines and infer the situation about which Paul writes.

The sad but inescapable conjecture that must be derived from Paul's writing in this chapter is that he had been subjected to a barrage of criticisms and attacks. As distasteful as it was to him, Paul felt constrained to show his credentials. Though it felt like boasting to him (and perhaps seems like it to us, as well) Paul was literally pleading for his own life and work as an apostle of Christ. Though it would have pleased him far more to spend his time extolling the virtues of Jesus Christ, he felt that he had to display his own virtues as the price of his privilege of preaching the gospel.

It is the custom in many churches to allow people to stand in their assembly of worship and make their testimony—to narrate their victories over sin and temptation and report the spiritual triumphs they have scored. Sometimes, the testimony becomes an exercise in boasting, meant to garner the sympathy or admiration of the listeners. But a true witness remembers to give glory where glory is due.

A seminary professor, teaching a class of young ministers-to-be, cautioned them that in preaching they should always "point to Jesus Christ, then get out of the way." Unfortunately, both requirements are difficult to fulfill. Whether we do our preaching from the pulpit or the pew, if we have seen some spiritual victory in our lives, it is hard not to let our fellow Christians know about it. But when Jesus admonished us to "let your light shine before others, so that they may see your good works," he completed the thought by saying, "and give glory to your Father in heaven" (Matthew 5:16).

Francis Parke Cadman, a distinguished minister of many years ago, was once called to a tenement apartment in the slum in New York City near where his church was located. A resident of the slum apartment was an elderly lady who lay dying. She had made her meager living for many years by scrubbing floors on her hands and knees. She was well known by the residents of the building where she worked, for she always had time to provide special courtesies for everyone. But she called for the minister to set before him her only fear about dying: "I'm not afraid to die," she said, "but I'm afraid I won't know what to say to God when I stand before the throne." The minister held her rough and callused hands and replied, "Don't say anything. Just show Him your hands."

The teaching set forth in this portion of Paul's letter may well contain the most helpful counsel the apostle ever penned to those who suffer. And there is not a person alive who does not need this counsel, for sorrow and suffering are the bequests of our humanity. We cannot avoid them, but the manner in which we deal with them will be the source of our greatest victory, or our greatest defeat.

Paul identifies his difficulty only as a "thorn in the flesh." Leaving its exact nature to our speculation has resulted in a host of conjectures. Some have speculated that Paul's trouble was spiritual: a recurring temptation that refused to be tamed, or a spiritual arrogance that resulted from his remarkable achievements, or persistent doubts that frequently undermined his belief system.

Others have suggested that the "thorn in the flesh" was some physical handicap or ailment that was painful, debilitating, and recurring. Perhaps it was some eye problem, which rendered him nearly blind and caused his severe headaches. Perhaps Paul's temporary blindness on the Damascus Road resulted in a residual problem with his eyes that was the mark of God's conquering of Paul. Or perhaps Paul's thorn in the flesh was a recurring fever, like malaria, which he might have contracted in his travels.

But it is to our benefit that we do not know the exact nature of Paul's thorn, because every one of us can identify with him. Each of us has his or her own thorn in the flesh, which may be visible to others or invisible. It may be spiritual or physical. It may be something we have brought on ourselves, or it may be an accident of chance. But whatever it is, it has two major symptoms: it hurts, and we can't conquer it.

Of course we can pray, and must! But even Paul prayed "three times," he says (but "three times" was idiomatic for "frequently"). And prayer always helps, but we don't always get the answer we hope for when we pray. Neither did Paul. But his prayer was answered. God's reply was not simply "no," but a qualified no: not what Paul wanted, but what he needed.

Fox's *Book of Martyrs* tells of a saint, many centuries ago, who was being held in a prison cell, awaiting his execution the next day for his faith. He was to be burned at the stake. In his loneliness in the dungeon his faith began to fail. "O Lord," he prayed, "give me grace to bear the fire." And the answer seemed to come to him, "No, today I give you grace to bear the fear. Tomorrow I will give you grace to bear the fire."

God's grace was sufficient for Paul, and it will be for you.

Among his concluding thoughts in this letter to the Corinthians, Paul exhorts his readers to "examine yourselves to see whether you are living in the faith" (v. 5a). It is such a simple idea that its wisdom is often overlooked. Consider the other aspects of our lives that we regularly subject to probative scrutiny. We arrange for a physical checkup to assure that our health is sound. We balance our checkbook to ensure that our finances are in order. We take refresher courses to sharpen our professional or vocational skills. We test the batteries in our smoke detectors at regular intervals. We do these things because we have learned, through painful experience, that unwatched assets can sometimes deteriorate and even disappear. To avoid that tragedy, we are wise enough to test what is important to us, to assure that it is still available to us when we really need it.

So Paul's injunction urges us to give the same verifying scrutiny to our spiritual lives. Our faith is, after all, a living thing, which means that either it grows or it dies. And the sad fact is that it doesn't make much noise when it does either. And many a person has come to the moment of one of life's urgent crises and has reached for his Christian faith, only to discover that his neglect has allowed it to wither and die.

Every now and then we should take the pulse of our convictions and measure the vitality of our passion for Christ. We become so engrossed with the road of life beneath our feet that we forget to look up, occasionally, to see where the road is leading. Ask yourself, "If I get where I'm going, where will I be? If I follow to its ending the path my feet are now treading, will I have gotten where I wanted to go? If I continue to develop the same qualities of character my present attitudes and behavior are leading me toward, will I wind up being what I wanted to become?" Such questions may be painful, because the answers may confront us with a stark and frightening fact: If we are not growing in our Christian faith, we are losing that battle. If Christ does not mean more to us than he did yesterday, we are losing our grip on him, and he is losing his grip on us. If our physical health is more important to us than our spiritual life, our body may be prospering, but our soul is dying.

Remember that, as Paul would say, the call of God to us is an "upward call." And you can't drift uphill!

At the end of a particularly trying day a kindergarten teacher slumped down in a chair in the teachers' lounge and asked her colleagues, "Do you know what teaching kindergarten is like?" Then she supplied the answer: "It's like trying to keep thirty-five corks under water at the same time!"

Surely Paul experienced the same sort of frustration with regard to his "children": those churches that he had established, and for which he felt a continuing responsibility. After founding each church and staying with it long enough to see it operating smoothly, he would leave it to begin a new work elsewhere. But in a short time reports would come to him that those churches that he left in good condition had developed problems. The church in Corinth had divided into competitive and hostile sects. The Thessalonians had accepted the belief in the imminent return of Christ as a license to default on all duties and responsibilities outside the church. If the end of the world was coming anyway, they reasoned, why work? Even his beloved Philippian congregation became the context of a church-sundering battle between two of its sisters.

Surely it was enough to try the patience of a saint. But Paul was not willing to accept the internal problems of his dear congregations without direct and remedial action. This he did in three ways: He returned for a personal visit when he was able to. Until that opportunity presented itself, he prayed earnestly for them. And he wrote them letters to help them solve their difficulty.

The following reflections will detail how Paul attempted to help the Galatians solve the problem that faced their church. But for today: Ask yourself if there are loved ones or friends whose troubles cause you concern. What are you doing to alleviate the problem? Don't say there's nothing you can do to help! At least, like Paul, you can pray for them and communicate your concern to them. No one was ever hurt by the discovery that someone cared about them and was praying for them.

"If something seems too good to be true, it usually is!" So runs the conventional wisdom. "You don't always get what you pay for, but you always pay for what you get!"

Who has not echoed a similar observation about life? "Something that costs nothing is worth exactly what it costs!" Despite the cynicism that underlies such remarks, most of us would agree that they are generally true. And it is that human mindset that makes it so difficult for some people to accept the good news of the Christian message. For the magnificent declaration of Christ's word is that our God does not conform to such minimalist expectations. No matter how good we may believe God is, God is never confined to our conclusions, but proceeds to deal with us with an astonishing generosity that puts all our miserly quid pro quos to shame.

Such a glorious understanding was beyond the timid reach of the faith of the Galatians—especially since the Judaizers were snapping at their heels with seemingly unimpeachable logic: "If the new Christian way no longer requires you to fulfill laws and perform rituals that Moses handed down, doesn't that prove that the Christian message is a fraud? Since when do shortcuts please God? A bargain-basement religion is worth only what it costs, which is nothing!"

But the Judaizers (and the Galatians who had been persuaded by them) did not understand that the new era of grace does not require of us less, but more! If a husband conscientiously fulfills all the laws delineating how he should treat his wife, he will be, in the end, involving himself in a great deal of painstaking research and accounting. But if he does only one thing, he can forget about all the laws: He can simply love his wife.

So we are no longer bound by law, but emancipated by grace. But if anyone thinks abiding by all the laws results in greater faithfulness than would be produced by love, that one has never really loved!

It is clear that Paul had great respect for the Old Testament Law, despite the fact that he regarded that law as having been fulfilled, and no longer the only means by which one might find favor with God. God provides for each person access to divine acceptance.

Paul reminds his readers that even though Abraham lived and died before the Mosaic Law was established, Abraham nevertheless found favor with God, because he believed in God, and expressed that belief in every way he knew to do so. So that was reckoned to him as righteousness.

But if Abraham had lived a few centuries later, after God had given the Law as a guide for living the kind of life that would please God, Abraham would have been subject to the dispensation of Law that was in effect at that time. Simple belief in God would not have been sufficient, once God had revealed a clearer and more detailed discipline.

So God had unfolded yet another flap on the map of continuing revelation. The Law—useful as it was at the time—was no longer the measuring stick by which God would determine one's fitness for companionship with God. The new covenant was one of grace— acceptance of God's unearned mercy. And once the new understanding is in effect, the old agreements are useful, but not binding.

Paul had an interesting way of putting it. He said "The law was our disciplinarian until Christ came, so that we might be justified by faith" (Galatians 3:24). The *King James Version* puts it even more lucidly: "The law was our schoolmaster to bring us unto Christ."

So one cannot ignore the law, even though we are not bound by it. No, it is not all right for us to commit murder or steal or do any of the other things forbidden by the old law. But our standard of conduct results not from law, but from love. "The love of Christ constrains us..." And that's a stronger stimulus than any law.

Having presented a rational argument against returning to the dispensation of law, Paul's continuing appeal to the perfidious Galatians now reveals how very deeply Paul cared for his readers, and how personally he regarded their defection. Paul rarely expressed affection for his readers, but in this chapter he calls them "my little children" (4:19) and speaks of them as though he had given them birth, even suffering the labor pains that normally accompany childbirth. This is the only instance in his writings when Paul employs the affectionate diminutive so often used by John: "my little children."

Again, Paul calls them "friends" ("brothers" in the original Greek). There is no question but that in this transition to personal pleas based on affection, Paul is providing an illustration of the truth he had been arguing: that God's appeal to us is not based on reason, but on affection—not on law, but on love.

Understood in this way, we can understand that betraying God and living contrary to the divine will is not so much a matter of breaking God's law, as it is a matter of breaking God's heart.

Though modern cynics might accuse Paul of "tear-jerking," Paul strengthened his personal appeal by reminding his Galatian readers of how much he had suffered for their sake, and how compassionately they had helped him through a crisis in his illness. For centuries Bible scholars have speculated about the exact nature of Paul's thorn in the flesh. There may be a hint in this chapter, when Paul says that when he came to them suffering his affliction, "had it been possible, you would have torn out your eyes and given them to me" (v. 15). Is it possible, as some have speculated, that Paul's experience of looking into the blazing light on the Road to Damascus left him visually impaired? If so, Paul's reference to their willingness to rip out their own eyes and give them to him would make sense.

In any case, Paul wants them to know that it was for them (and the others of the Gentile world to whom Paul believes God sent him) that he suffered that affliction—a cross he would bear for the rest of his life.

It was on this basis that Paul's personal appeal was made. And in this he reflects the love of Christ, dying on the cross as the cost of our redemption. As someone once said, "Jesus was asked, 'How much do you love me?' And he stretched out his hands and said, 'This much!' and died."

Carl Sandburg, in one of his poems, pictured the perennial problem posed by his unruly instincts, and expressed that problem symbolically by saying he had a whole menagerie under his ribs. "I am a pal of the earth," he said, "I am come from the wilderness." We know, all too well, what he meant. There is a bit of wild, untamed animal nature in every one of us. An old poem by Edward Sandford Martin called "Mixed" says it this way:

> Within my earthly temple there's a crowd.
> There's one of us that's humble; one that's proud.
> There's one that's broken-hearted for his sins,
> And one who, unrepentant, sits and grins...
> From much corroding care would I be free
> If once I could determine which is Me!

Unfortunately, that spiritual schizophrenia does not end when we become Christians. As much as we may welcome the freedom from the old law, we must constantly be aware of the danger that such freedom presents. Our battle with temptation is never permanently won, even with the spirit of Christ residing within us. Even the Savior faced his recurrent struggle against the lure of compromise with baser inclinations. Gethsemane was proof of that.

But if our Christian discipleship offers us freedom from the bondage of law, it also provides for us the means by which we may be victorious in our battle to be our best selves. That secret weapon in the Christian's arsenal is the Holy Spirit—God's active presence in our lives. But in order for the spirit to accomplish the work of producing in us the fruits of Christlikeness, we must keep our reverent attention focused on that Spirit.

"The road to hell is paved with good intentions" runs the old proverb. But so is the road to heaven! And whether our earthly nature or our spiritual nature wins the battle for possession of our souls depends upon which nature receives our deliberate, disciplined intent. And if we hospitably welcome the spirit of God into our lives, and nourish that spirit by our willing compliance with its heavenly urges, we will produce all those fruits of the spirit that Paul said are the fingerprints of the spirit.

Like Jesus, Paul tailored his message to the experience and understanding of his readers. His masterful stories reflected the life and occupations with which they were familiar. He spoke of fishing boats and nets, and of shepherds and their flocks, and of homemakers and their daily chores.

So Paul, writing to people who lived in an agrarian society in the rural area of Galatia, created one of his most memorable teachings in a figure with which his readers would immediately identify. Their experience with sowing and reaping had taught them the inviolable principles of their craft. If they wanted a crop of wheat, they must sow wheat seeds. Even the most diligent nurture could not make wheat seeds produce a bumper crop of corn! If one wanted wheat, one had to plant wheat seeds.

But Paul–wonderfully practical Paul–reminded them that even the proper seed did not immediately produce the desired crop. Between sowing and harvesting there had to be much backbreaking labor, and the contributions of sunlight and moisture only God could provide. And even with all the requisite elements in place, time had to play its essential role. One cannot hurry nature's processes.

So Paul reminded his readers that the Christian character requires the proper investment of our effort and faith. You cannot make a fool out of God! You cannot sow one thing and reap another. You cannot sow unrighteous thoughts and actions and reap sainthood!

But even with all the proper ingredients in place, farming still requires the patience to let the miracle of growth take place. So those who work with the soil know that they cannot abandon their hoeing and weeding when the sun grows hot and the weeds invade. They must continue to work even when their efforts seem unblessed by success.

So in our cultivation of the Christian character, there comes a time when all our efforts seem unfruitful. Temptation still plagues us. Neighbors sipping lemonade under a shade tree may ridicule our faith and the labor it calls for. But if we keep doing what we know is right, eventually we will be blessed with a harvest. "In due season," Paul said, "we shall reap" (v. 9, KJV). Sometimes that "due season" seems the longest season of the year. But as surely as God is God, the harvest will come. And that's a certainty you can carry with you all through the long desert stretches between faith and reward.

DAY 80

Paul's epistle to the Ephesians is, in the opinion of many scholars, the supreme effort on the part of the great apostle to define the Christian faith. It was clearly not intended to solve some pressing immediate problem or to give instructions regarding some aspect of church life. It was, rather, his most systematic and thoughtful statement of the faith, gleaned through years of experience, clarified by careful study and prayer.

Despite many nagging mysteries that defy our most diligent efforts to find solutions, there are some facts about which we can be reasonably certain. First, it seems abundantly clear that Paul was writing this letter toward the end of his magnificently productive ministry, and that he was writing this masterpiece while in prison!

One might forgive Paul if he had written into this letter his frustrations and resentments. There was so much more he had wanted to do. He had spoken of his dreams of going to Spain to bring the good news of Christ to those who had not had the opportunity to hear the gospel proclaimed. He had dreamed of returning to some places where he had established churches, to bring them comfort as they faced persecution and the incursion of persistent heresies. But there he was, sick, old, frustrated by failing eyesight and left to die in a lonely prison cell. But his gallant and unconquerable spirit vaulted over the walls and through the bars of his prison to bring light to a dark world—a spirit that has continued for twenty centuries to inspire and instruct. Surely Paul turned his limiting circumstances into the most challenging opportunity of his entire life!

Paul would certainly have understood and sympathized with your limitations. But he would surely point out to you that whatever circumstances frustrate you, there is, within your limitations, an opportunity to serve God and bless the world.

In a private interview with Bishop K. H. Ting of China—one of the world's greatest Christian leaders—the author noted the challenging limitations within which the Christians of China must practice their faith. But the elderly saint, instead of railing against the government for placing such restrictions on the work of the church, answered gently, "So the question becomes, 'How well are we using the space we are given?'" That is the question for all of us!

During the Second World War a small group of American soldiers brought to a small church the body of a comrade who had fallen in battle. They wanted to give him a Christian burial, and asked the priest if they could lay their friend to rest in the cemetery adjacent to the chapel. The priest asked if their friend had been a Catholic. They replied sadly that they did not know. "I'm sorry," the priest replied, "but the rules are clear. Only those baptized in the Catholic Church can be buried in hallowed ground."

The soldiers turned to leave in sorrow. But the priest offered a compromise. "I cannot bury him in hallowed ground, but you can inter his body just outside the fence." This the friends did.

Many years later, after the war, the soldiers made a return trip to France where the burial had taken place. They went to a spot just outside the fence where their memory directed them, but found no such burial site. In their disappointment they sought out the priest and asked him what had happened to their friend's grave. The priest answered, "The night after your visit I could not sleep because of my refusal to allow your friend to be buried in hallowed ground. I knew that the rules had to be obeyed. But the next morning I went out and moved the fence to include the body of your friend."

Such is the love of Christ, which brings alienated people together. He abolished the rule of law and instituted the reign of grace. "He is our peace," Paul said (v. 14). And when we allow the spirit of Christ to come into the "no man's land" between alienated peoples, the differences between members of God's family are dissolved.

In the mountains that mark the boundary between Chile and Argentina, there is a towering statue of Jesus known as "The Christ of the Andes." It was erected at a time when frequent border disputes between the two countries erupted in violence. But the people of both countries, disheartened by their inability to create peace through their own efforts, erected that statue, so that thereafter when the people of each country looked upon the residents of the other, they saw the Christ standing between them.

Think what it would do to all your broken relationships if you could always think of Christ standing between you and that one whom you cannot seem to love.

DAY 82
Read Ephesians 3

To mark the end of this first section of the letter, Paul offers his doxology of praise to God, and concludes with one of the most graceful benedictions to be found anywhere. He writes, "To him who by the power at work within us is able to accomplish abundantly far more than all we could ask or imagine, to him be glory..." (3:20).

Packed within those timeless words are two astonishing realizations: first, that it is through us that God intends to fulfill the holy purpose of creation, and, second, that this unconquerable power is already loosed within us and—pending our willingness to be the host of such achievements—is aiming for such triumphs as we can scarcely imagine.

An Indian mystic tells that he once observed on the streets of Calcutta such tragic evidences of poverty that he was moved to cry out to God, "Lord, how can you allow such human misery? Why don't you do something about it?" The mystic was stunned to hear the voice of God within him saying, "I have done something about it! I made you!"

If we wonder why God is so slow in recreating the world to conform to the dimensions of the kingdom of heaven, we must realize that the answer lies within us. God has already given us all the tools we need to accomplish that work. But those tools have become rusty from disuse.

Make no mistake about this: The power God sets to work in us is intended to achieve God's divine purpose. If you are doing what God wants done, God will not suffer your efforts to fail. But if you insist on working contrary to God's purpose, the whole universe will oppose your efforts.

Sometimes we are disappointed in ourselves, ashamed of what we have done, as though something had gotten into us that made us conduct ourselves at a level below our own hopes and expectations. "The devil made me do it!" we say, recalling the theme often employed by a comedian of a few years ago. But when we rise above our own inclinations and surprise ourselves by a magnanimity that lies beyond our usual performance, is it not possible that "God is at work in us"?

And as a master carpenter reaches most often for those tools that have proven the most effective in achieving the workman's purpose, so God will turn, again and again, to those people whose lives hasten the coming of the heavenly kingdom. If you want God's power to work in you, make sure God's investment of resources is not wasted on you.

Five-year-old Justin was attending his first day of first grade, having completed his kindergarten year the previous spring. When noontime came he was tired, and, remembering his previous experience with mornings-only kindergarten, he gathered up his belongings and headed for the door. The teacher met him at the back door and asked where he was going. "I'm going home," he replied. The teacher gently explained that in first grade the sessions would continue until 4:00. With a mixture of disappointment and indignation, he placed his hands on his hips and demanded, "Well, who the heck signed me up for this?"

Poor Justin had just learned an important fact about life: Each stage of our growth carries with it additional responsibility. And Christian discipleship is no exception. Although we celebrate the gift of grace, which makes our discipleship possible in the first place, we must assume the responsibilities implied by our acceptance of that gift. To put Paul's teaching in the simplest possible terms, if we are Christians, we must act like it!

Unfortunately, though the Christian life is possible, it is never easy. Paul says "making every effort" is an essential ingredient. Three times in this chapter he begins a sentence by saying "you must": "You must no longer be children"..."You must grow up"..."You must no longer live as the Gentiles." And in numerous other expressions Paul makes it quite clear that the Christian life cannot result from our effort, but is not possible without it.

The apostle closes this section by saying, "Do not grieve the Holy Spirit of God." The Holy Spirit is the divine presence working within us that points us in the right direction and gives us a shove. When we are very young our parents fulfill this role for our lives, instructing us about what is right and what is wrong, and giving us a start in the right direction. They cannot compel us to conform to their standards of conduct, but if we live contrary to their standards, we hurt and disappoint them. We may be said to "grieve the hearts" of our parents.

So even the great God cannot compel us to live in a way that is right for us and pleasing to God. But God does everything short of countermanding our freedom of choice. God gives us the direction of the Holy Word, and of the Word made flesh, and of the continuing presence of the Holy Spirit within us. But if, despite all that, we deliberately choose the wrong way, God grieves for us, even as human parents grieve for their wayward children. It is not so much a matter of breaking God's law, as it is a matter of breaking God's heart.

DAY 84

The society in which Paul and his readers lived was a stratified society, in which one's status mandated the courtesy and respect to be accorded to that person. There was a "pecking order" that controlled social relationships. Romans were given a higher place in society than Greeks; men outranked women; adults ruled children; the rich were given greater deference than the poor. But Paul insisted that in Christ all people deserve equal respect.

Such was the message that Jesus had sent by way of his own example. He cut across all the rules of his society by giving his courteous attention to a sinful woman of a despised country whom he met at a well. He interrupted the triumphal entry into Jerusalem to honor the little children who clamored for his notice. He spent some of his last breaths to attend to a request hurled at him from a convicted felon who shared his crucifixion. He saw every person as worthy of his concern. This was because Jesus was able to recognize the divine imprint on every soul. "The kingdom of God is among you," he said to an astonished audience (Luke 17:21).

And since every person—of any age or race or gender or character—is a child of God, and one upon whom God is depending to establish the reign of heaven on earth, that person is deserving of our genuine respect.

"Love me, love my dog" runs an admonition that was once frequently heard. And if there is some validity in that exhortation, think how much more valid is the charge: "If you love me, you will love my child." We are justifiably offended by anyone who would claim to love us if they despise our sons or daughters.

So God demands of us, "If you love me, you will love my child." And every person qualifies for that respect. An immigrant from Ireland was boasting about the new society he had found in his adopted America. "In this country," he said, "every man is as good as his neighbor. And, for that matter, a little better."

So Paul says, "Be subject to one another out of reverence for Christ." Since our Christ died for every person, we must show our reverence for Christ by sharing his magnificent obsession: that every person is as deserving of our esteem as any other. And for that matter, a little more.

It was a dangerous age in which Paul lived. Human life was cheap, and there were few protections. Not many people could afford the kind of residence that would withstand the ravages of nature or the malignant intent of thieves. Disease and death reigned where good nutrition and inadequate sanitation were unknown. Except for a few elite members of the ruling class, life itself depended, from day to day, upon the whim of the government. Life was uncertain, and death was inevitable.

In that anxious world one figure stood out as a personification of security. It was the Roman soldier—a familiar figure in every city and town throughout the Roman Empire. He strode with the confidence of one who knew that he was supported and protected by the greatest power in the world: the Roman Empire. Wherever he went, he knew that all the resources of the empire would defend him against all enemies. And his military uniform represented the latest word in personal protection. His body was encased in armor; he had a breastplate to protect his vital organs. He carried a shield in one hand, and a sword in the other. Surely every boy growing up in that era looked in envious admiration at that picture of confident safety.

It is that picture of security in an insecure world that Paul says is suggestive of the manner in which our Christian faith defends us. Our faith in God is our sure defense. And though empires may rise and fall, the power of God is eternal. And "if God is for us, who is against us?" Paul asked in his Roman letter (Romans 8:31). "We are more than conquerors through him who loved us" (Romans 8:37).

Picture Jesus hanging on the cross. His enemies seem to have won. He is suffering a horrible death; his work apparently has been wasted; his friends and loved ones seem to be without comfort, without hope. But Jesus, in supreme confidence, said, among his last words, "Father, into your hands I commend my spirit" (Luke 23:46). His enemies might torture his body, but what meant the most to him—his soul, his integrity, his spirit, his very life—were in hands that were loving and strong, hands that would not fail, then or ever! Earth has no haven as secure as that!

DAY 86

Read Philippians 1

In the early days of the twentieth century there was a comedian known as "Uncle Josh." His routines (remembered because some of them were recorded on cylinders) seem a bit naïve to us but always had a moral point, which is more than we have come to expect of modern comedy. In one of his routines, he tells about a farmer uncle of his who had an old mule that had outlived its usefulness and was an expensive nuisance to keep around. So the uncle decided to put the old critter out of his misery. He dropped the mule down a dry well, thinking the fall itself would surely kill him. But when the farmer looked down the shaft, he saw those old eyes looking up at him reproachfully, accusingly. So the farmer saw that to finish the job, he would have to bury the mule in the well. So he brought wagonload after wagonload of dirt and dumped them into the well, on top of the mule. Finally, when the last wagonload was dumped in, the mule, which had methodically put each succeeding wagonload of dirt under his feet, calmly surmounted the last load, and serenely walked out of the well onto dry ground. He had taken what was meant to bury him and used it as a ladder to reach victory.

That is pretty much what Paul had done, and in his letter to the Philippians he claimed that achievement, and encouraged his readers to aim at the same strategy. His principle, based upon his own experience, was that if you truly want what God wants, God will make it possible for you to use anything and everything that happens to you to raise you higher and higher until victory is within your reach. And when you know that is going to happen, you will have hope and joy all along the way—even when the dirt starts falling on your head.

In the Old Testament story of Joseph this principle may be seen. His envious brothers sold him into slavery, thinking they had seen the last of him. But as Joseph later realized, "God intended it for good" (Genesis 50:20). God was up to something in Joseph's life.

How God must have chuckled the day that Saul of Tarsus was stopped cold in his tracks on the way to Damascus, knowing what was going to be accomplished in that unlikely life. God was up to something in the life of Saul, as well.

But God was up to something in the lives of the Philippian Christians, too. And Paul assured them that the same God, who had used both the bad and the good to make marvelous results in his life, would do the same for them, if they were going God's way.

Read Philippians 2

Paul respected the differences between human beings. God made us all, and made none of us exactly like anyone else who ever lived. But what you are and what you have must blend with all the other different people and their widely varying understandings and abilities and gifts, in order for the church to be everything it is supposed to be, everywhere it exists. So how can the church achieve this harmony and unity without destroying the richness of our diversity?

This was the solution Paul provided the Philippians in the second chapter of his epistle. He first asked them to consider Christ, our perfect model. Do you think you have the Holy Spirit? You surely cannot claim to be more in possession of God's presence than Jesus was. Do you think you understand Christian doctrine and theology, and that you have studied the scriptures until you know all of God's truth? You cannot claim to know more about the Word of God than Jesus, who was the Word made flesh. And do you really think your prayer life is superior to Christ's? He lived in constant companionship with God. And would you be so presumptuous as to say that your commitment to the good of others, your dedication to service is superior to his? He gave his life for the salvation of the world.

Then Paul says (and ponder this!): This Spirit-filled, theologically correct, sacrificial, full-of-faith, morally perfect human being–who was also God–did not consider any of these qualifications as worthy of boasting about, but poured it all out for the good of others.

Then listen to Paul's word: "Let the same mind be in you that was in Christ Jesus, who, though he was in the form of God, did not regard equality with God as something to be exploited, but emptied himself, taking the form of a slave" (vv. 5–7a). In other words, he who had every right to flex his spiritual muscles and throw his divine weight around laid it all on the altar of love, and saved the world.

It is worth noting that Jesus earned the veneration in which he is held, not by having all those gifts, but in pouring them all out in concern for the world. So it is not what we have, but what we give that makes us most like him.

DAY 88
Read Philippians 3

Paul's great statement of personal strategy begins with the phrase "forgetting what lies behind" (v. 13). Those words make use of an idiom that says, literally, "shaking loose." Something of that same meaning is preserved in certain words in our language, like the word "solution." When you find a solution for a problem, that means that you have shaken it loose. And when you make a New Year's resolution, the word literally means, "shaken loose again." Before you can take a new and different direction, you have to shake loose whatever clings to you that has kept you traveling in the old rut.

In this symbolic sense, that's what Jesus kept saying to people around him: "You must let go of all the garbage that you have accumulated through the years—all that unnecessary baggage that includes your prejudices, your resentments, your fears, your disappointments, which have made you cynical. You must shake loose your hurts, which have calloused your mind and heart to protect you from further hurt. You must even shake loose your past successes, which have given you an inflated sense of your own wisdom and a distrustfulness of anybody else's. Shake them all loose. Turn them all over to God, and trust God to put into your empty hands and hearts all the good things you really need."

Again and again in the gospels we read of people who took Jesus at his word, and in a phrase used so often in the New Testament, "they left all and followed him." They shook loose the old life, to begin the new.

There is a lovely saying that "every saint has a past, and every sinner has a future." In either case, that is possible only by "shaking loose" the residue of our past that clings to us like beggar lice. Think of the old poem:

As children bring their broken toys with tears, for us to mend,
I brought my broken dreams to God, because he was my friend.
But then, instead of leaving him in peace to work alone,
I hung around and tried to help, in ways that were my own.
At last I snatched them back and cried, "How can you be so slow?"
"My child," God said, "what could I do? You never did let go."

DAY 89
Read Philippians 4

Paul's primary purpose in writing this gracious letter to the congregation at Philippi was to thank them for the gift of money they had sent him. Paul was in prison in Rome, and it was the custom of the day for the friends and families of those jailed to provide for their food and clothing and other simple necessities. The jailers felt no such obligation. So it was literally to keep Paul from starving to death that members of the Philippian church passed the hat, and sent the offering to Paul.

Paul's gracious acknowledgment of their gift, with which he closes the letter, is one of the most beautiful passages in the New Testament, and tells us a great deal not only about his friendship with the Philippian Christians but also about Paul's attitude toward needs and wants, and about money and possessions. Listen to these words of his:

"I know what it is to have little, and I know what it is to have plenty. In any and all circumstances I have learned the secret of being well-fed and of going hungry, of having plenty and of being in need. I can do all things through him who strengthens me" (vv. 12–13). In subsequent verses he says, "I…have more than enough; I am fully satisfied…And my God will satisfy every need of yours according to his riches in glory in Christ Jesus" (vv. 18, 19).

There is a simple honesty and innocent joy in Paul's statement. "In fact," Paul says, to everyone's amazement, "I am rich!"

But even more astonishing is Paul's confident promise that God will make us rich too! Perhaps the question is, what would it take to make you rich? For being rich is not dependent upon bank accounts and the Dow Jones average. Rather, being rich is having what is most important to you. If all you want is money—or all the things money will buy—then you will never be rich enough. There is a chronic dissatisfaction built into all material rewards, which is precisely why the richer you get, the richer you feel the need to be. There is a bumper sticker slogan that says, "Never too rich, never too thin," which provides a cynical commentary on the futility of seeking only material wealth.

How rich will you feel if, at some dust-settling time in your life, what you want most is peace of mind, or the ability to look at yourself in the mirror without flinching, or release from guilt, or some hope to hold on to when death stares you in the face? If, at such a time, you have the confidence of knowing that "my God will supply all your need," then you'll be rich, too.

DAY 90
Read Colossians 1

The pastor of the church woke up one Sunday morning to discover that a case of laryngitis had left him without a voice. Who would lead the service and preach the sermon at the morning worship service? After a moment of prayerful thought he phoned a friend of his, a respected elder in the congregation. He struggled, in his hoarse whisper, to explain the problem and to plead for the elder's help. Without hesitation the elder agreed to fill in for the minister.

In a simple and straightforward manner the elder presented to the congregation the modest but practical method he used when he read the Bible. "I always ask myself three questions when I read anything in the Bible: First, do you know what it says? Second, do you understand what it means? And third, are you willing to do what it demands?"

It would be difficult to conceive a more effective way to get inside a scripture passage and appropriate it for one's life. The leap between "knowing" and "understanding" is surpassed in importance only by the gulf between "understanding" and "doing."

Paul attempts to help the Colossian Christians bridge that important gulf in his prayer, "that you may be filled with the *knowledge* of God's will in all spiritual wisdom and *understanding,* so that you may *lead lives* worthy of the Lord" (vv. 9–10a). Knowing the will of God is not enough; neither is understanding what it means. It is only when we complete the circuit by appropriating the truth of the Word into our lives that God's power becomes available to us.

A farmer was once called upon by a traveling salesman who attempted to lure the farmer into the purchase of certain agricultural equipment. "Don't you want to know how to be a better farmer?" the salesman asked. "Heck," the farmer replied, "I already know that. What I need is the gumption to do what I know."

Today, take one sentence of scripture. Read it carefully, to make sure you know what it says. Then pray for God's help in understanding what it means. Finally, whatever it costs, do what it asks of you.

DAY 91
Read Colossians 2

There is a little sentence in this chapter that should leap off the printed page and confront every Christian in this secular age. It says, "If with Christ you died to the elemental spirits of the universe, why do you live as if you still belonged to the world?" (v. 20). It is difficult, these days, to see much difference between the lifestyle of the Christians and those who claim no such distinction.

It is most unfortunate that one of our great hymns of consecration is usually listed in our hymnals by an abbreviation of the first line that negates the thought intended by the writer. So "Take my life and let it be consecrated, Lord, to thee" becomes "Take My Life and Let It Be." Tragically, that self-contained contradiction reflects the mincing compromise that passes for commitment in many a Christian's life. We want the privileges and blessings of the Christian lifestyle, so we plead, "Take my life," but when it comes to offering any real surrender to the way of Christ, we demur, "but let it be." Let my life alone, Lord! I'll give you my words and my good intentions, but don't expect any real demonstration of my faith to be revealed in the way I live.

Paul frequently warned his readers against such "elemental spirits" as hedonism—the worship of the flesh. "If it feels good, do it" is the theme song of the hedonists, and there are many today who sing that song with genuine fervor. But as Christians we cannot afford such a cowardly surrender to our baser desires.

Materialism, too, is a repudiation of the Christian spirit. But what does it say about our rejection of that worldly standard if we lay more of our gifts at the foot of this idol than what we put into the offering plate to express our dedication to Christ?

The world respects aggressiveness and competitiveness. "It's a dog-eat-dog world out there," we say. And Jesus strictly ruled out that behavior that tramples our neighbors under the foot of our ambition. "So shall it not be among you," Jesus warned his disciples when they exhibited such arrogance (Mark 10:43, KJV). But is it so among us?

An old popular song said, "Your lips tell me no, no; but there's yes, yes in your eyes." So your lips may say you are a follower of Christ. But what does your lifestyle say?

"Remember who you are!" So runs the familiar exhortation with which parents frequently challenge their offspring to conduct that will honor their family tradition. It was in that same spirit that Paul reminded the Colossian Christians of their identity. You are "God's chosen ones," Paul tells them. You are "holy and beloved" (v. 12). Note that these extravagant qualifications were given to the Colossians as gifts. They were not the achievements of the readers. God had chosen them, and had given them the distinction of sainthood (which comes from the same source as the word "holy"). Their "holiness" meant "useful to God," just as the holy temple or the holy altar had no saintly qualities, but were made holy because they were useful to God.

But Paul also reminds his readers that they are loved by God. What an effect that knowledge must have had upon them, to know that God loved them! How could they possibly live in the knowledge that the great God of the universe cared, personally, about them, without some resulting effect upon them? Wouldn't that make some difference in your life, if you were in constant remembrance of that?

So Paul proceeds to describe some of the aspects of the life that should be lived by those who know God loves them. And the surprising thing is that Paul indicates that this enormous debt we owe to God must be paid in the daily coin of love and forbearance toward other people. We are to bear with one another patiently, and forgive one another, and above all, we are to manifest toward others the kind of love Christ expressed toward us when he made his supreme sacrifice on our behalf.

At a training conference for workers with children, each of the participants was asked to wear a nametag, which proclaimed in large letters, "I am a child of God. Treat me that way!"

If you know you are loved by God, and that God loves other people as well, shouldn't that make some difference in the manner in which you act toward all other people? Remember who you are!

Prayer, for many people, is like the emperor's new clothes, which, according to the charlatans in the fairy tale of that name, could be seen and appreciated only by those who were pure in heart. But when nobody could see the "new clothes" that the emperor was supposedly wearing, each was afraid to confess that he couldn't see them, for fear he would only be revealing his own guilty conscience. But it took an innocent child to point out the truth: "The emperor has nothing on!"

So we hide our doubts about the efficacy of prayer behind our guilty consciences, but we find some comfort in hearing pure-minded children express their own misgivings about prayer. Like the little girl who remained kneeling silently at her bedside for several minutes while her watchful parents kept waiting for her prayers to begin. When they prompted her to start her prayers, she complained, "But I can't seem to get waited on." But there is a hollow ring to our laughter, because we recall, all too painfully, those times when we took some urgent request to God, and we couldn't seem to get waited on either.

Nevertheless, the whole Bible, from beginning to end, maintains that God always hears, and will always answer our prayers. God says, "Call to me and I will answer you." No qualifications, no strings attached, no footnotes claiming exemptions, just a simple divine promise, "Call to me and I will answer."

There is not a letter of Paul's that lacks his urging to be faithful in prayer. And in this closing chapter of his letter to the church at Colossae, he urges, "Devote yourselves to prayer, keeping alert in it" (4:2). But how can we be faithful and diligent in our prayer life when we often feel that God has ignored our prayers? Perhaps it is because we expect the wrong result from our prayers. The primary consequence of our prayers is a closer relationship with God. Often people say, "I don't pray because God does not seem real to me." Rather, they should say, "God does not seem real to me because I do not pray."

But God always answers our prayers. The answer is not always "yes"; sometimes the answer, in God's greater wisdom and love for us, is "no." And the hardest answer of all for us to accept is "wait." But those are answers, too. If we persist in prayer, we may be sure God will answer in the way God knows is best for us.

As was the case with most of his other letters, Paul penned this epistle to the church at Thessalonica to help them deal with problems that had arisen in their corporate life. But Paul was a faithful practitioner of the "stroke before you poke" strategy in pointing out flaws. He always began by recognizing the virtues and accomplishments of his readers before taking them to task for their flaws. So in the entire first chapter of this letter there is not a single hint of Paul's displeasure with them. He first recognized and acknowledged their many qualities and achievements that were worthy of praise.

Lest someone think this strategy is only a vapid congregational gimmick, remember that Jesus believed in giving credit where credit was due, and criticized those who went through life seeing only the faults and mistakes of others. "Why do you see the specks?" he asked. To be sure it is easy to see the specks in the world around us, for this is, after all, a speckled world. To see the specks proves only that you are reasonably intelligent. But to see only the specks proves that you are unreasonably critical.

So Paul celebrates the virtues in that very human congregation before dealing with their problems. And there was much about that church to be celebrated. It was the first church to be established on the continent of Europe, although Paul was able to remain there only three weeks before being chased out of town by an angry mob. Surely with such a brief opportunity to preach the gospel and establish a congregation, and remembering Paul's unceremonious departure at the insistence of an angry mob, it was a bit much to hope that the church in that city would have survived and thrived. But such had been the case. And for that alone the Thessalonians deserved praise.

And beyond that, the church had served as a model for other new congregations and had been impelled by the missionary spirit to send out Christian emissaries to other places. Paul was entirely right in his approach: whatever their problems, there was much about them that was deserving of praise.

How it would improve our lives and our society if we always followed Paul's "stroke before you poke" pattern. Before you are tempted to condemn or criticize anyone, try taking an inventory of his or her virtues, and give thanks for them and show gratitude for them. If you are honest in that process, you may discover—long before you get around to mentioning them—that the flaws you intended to hold up for scorn had disappeared.

The warm personal tribute to the Thessalonians that filled the first chapter continues in the second chapter, though with a subtle, sad difference. Beneath the affectionate references, in which he speaks of himself as their father, or as their nursemaid, there begin to surface some of the reasons for the letter. In reading between the lines, we can discern some of the slanderous remarks that had been made against him.

There were those who accused Paul of being mentally deluded. The gospel he preached was obviously too good to be true. So, their logic concluded, he had to be mad. This was neither the first nor the last time that Paul would be thought demented. Festus said to him, "You are out of your mind, Paul! Too much learning is driving you insane!" (Acts 26:24). But Paul didn't mind such a charge. In fact, he was able to say, "Let no one think that I am a fool; but if you do, then accept me as a fool, so that I too may boast a little" (2 Corinthians 11:16). It was not his own reputation Paul cared about, but Christ's.

Apparently there were others accusing Paul of preaching a message intended to draw the praise of people. They thought his gospel of grace, which released people from the bondage of law, made religion too easy. "If it's more pleasant, it must be false," they reasoned. "Everyone knows that real religion is difficult and costly." But even Jesus had said, "Come unto me all you that are weary and are carrying heavy burdens, and I will give you rest" (Matthew 11:28). And Jesus said those words to people who were weary of carrying the heavy burdens of the multitude of laws imposed upon them by their religion. If Paul's preaching won the praise of people, it was because it was wonderfully good news.

Others accused Paul of being in the ministry for personal reward, either material or social, or because it gave him a position of prestige and authority. There must have been a multitude of complaints and criticisms against one whose gifts and character gave him such a prominent place in his world. But, as the saying goes, "You'll always find the most clubs under the tree with the most apples on it." And Paul's monumental contributions had to be made at the cost of persevering against the assaults of the cynical, the narrow-minded, the provincial, the mean-spirited, the obstinate, and the tradition-bound.

But so did Jesus'. And when you are subjected to unwarranted vituperation, take comfort in the words of Jesus, "Woe to you when all speak well of you" (Luke 6:26).

At least Paul did not have to worry about that problem! And neither should we!

It is clear that the church at Thessalonica had a very special place in Paul's heart. It was the first church planted on the European continent, and Paul obviously intended the work there as a kind of beachhead for the gospel in a new world. As Paul had said at the conclusion of the previous chapter, "You are our glory and joy!"

But now Paul was separated from Thessalonica by a great distance. Although he had heard no negative reports about the church he had established, his separation from them and his deep affection for them gave birth to the kinds of anxieties we feel about any loved one from whom we are separated by a great distance. After all, he had spent only three weeks in their presence, establishing the new congregation, and he knew only too well the perils that confront new believers.

Paul expressed his concern by sending his assistant, Timothy, back to Thessalonica, instead of keeping the young man with him as he faced one of the most difficult tasks in his entire ministry: preaching the gospel in the world's capital of paganism, Athens. Silas and Luke had also been left at Berea to supervise the work of the new congregation there, so Paul was utterly alone when he went to Athens and his most severe challenge (and what was apparently his most grievous loss). But Paul was willing to make that sacrifice because of his love and concern for the Thessalonians.

In this magnanimous and sacrificial proof of his love for the Christians at Thessalonica, Paul was mirroring the great redemptive act of God. "God proves his love for us in that while we still were sinners Christ died for us" (Romans 5:8). God cared enough to send the very best! Imagine the effect this demonstration of affection and sacrifice had upon the Thessalonian Christians! How could they possibly fail, when they knew that the great apostle himself was willing to make a costly sacrifice to assure that they remained faithful?

Does that say anything to you about your importance? Whatever your faults and however minimal your contributions to the kingdom, you are a person for whom Christ died. Knowing that, how can you live as those do who have received no such evidence of divine approbation?

DAY 97
Read 1 Thessalonians 4

In a charming display of tact (which Paul sometimes lacked in dealing with the sins of his Christian readers) he urges the Thessalonians, "You ought to live and to please God (as, in fact, you are doing), [but] you should do so more and more" (v. 1). What exactly did that mean? Did they please God by their conduct? Then how could they be expected to "do so more and more"? Isn't morality an absolute standard, to which one either conforms or not?

We must remember that the Thessalonians lived in a particularly hedonistic age. Even the prevailing religion depicted the gods themselves as indulging in all kinds of immoral behavior. When Christianity came to Thessalonica it brought with its belief system a new moral code that was as strange and different to the Thessalonians as a foreign language would have been. And while they had accepted this new moral code, they continued to live in the midst of a society in which the old immorality was the coin of the realm.

Was their progress toward the Christian ideal a bit slow at times? Did some of the new Christians occasionally backslide into the old ways? Were there times when the Christians were tempted to wonder if their new faith was worth the sacrifice it demanded? It is probable that such was the case.

But though it was painfully slow and inconsistent, their growth toward the Christian ideal was encouraging enough to please God.

How refreshing to discover that God does not demand perfection of us, and will not repudiate any effort of ours that may not achieve absolute conformity with the holy will. The fact is that the Thessalonians were pleasing God by the manner in which they lived. Can the same be said of us?

Once in a testimonial meeting at church, an old lady rose to give her witness: "I ain't what I ought to be, and I ain't what I could be, but the Lord knows I ain't what I used to be, and I'm marchin'!" I think God would have approved.

DAY 98
Read 1 Thessalonians 5

About the second coming of Christ there has been endless speculation, despite the fact that Jesus himself warned against such futile conjecturing. Even during his ministry, he was frequently confronted with such questions, and he invariably answered that no one knew when that day would be, that even he did not know, and that it was both irreverent and vain for human beings to try to take out of God's hands what has been reserved for God's own province (see Mark 13:32; Matthew 24:36, and Acts 1:7). Still the speculation continues, even in our day.

It should be enough for us to know that (1) Jesus did, indeed, indicate that he would return at some point in time, to bring to final fulfillment the purpose for which earth was created; (2) that it would come unexpectedly, to everyone's surprise; and that (3) it would be a time of judgment for every human being.

Some theologians have argued for a "realized eschatology"–that Christ's coming again has already happened, either through his resurrection from the dead, or through the coming of the Holy Spirit on Pentecost. Most, however, feel that the cosmic event that Jesus believed would happen is yet to come, though when and how are questions that no human being can answer.

Obviously, the one thing we can–and must–do is to keep ourselves ready at all times for the coming of Christ. Even if the second coming of Christ is an event that will not occur for many eons to come, there will come a time for each of us when we shall meet him in the experience of death. Of that day and hour we have no knowledge. But we do know that it is coming, that it will be a surprise, and that it will bring an experience of judgment.

An old Scotsman lay dying. His daughter, thinking he might want to hear a reading from the scriptures, asked, "Father, shall I bring the book?" "Nay, lassie," he replied, "I thatched my roof before the storms came."

Those who have carefully thatched their roof need not fear the storm. And those who live, day by day, as they would want to be found when their last day comes, need not fear the judgment.

DAY 99
Read 2 Thessalonians 1

Here, again, is striking evidence of the tender tact of which Paul was so capable, though he did not always utilize it. Apparently a report had come to Paul (a letter, perhaps, or a firsthand report from Timothy, whom Paul had sent to Thessalonica) in which the young Christians of that congregation had expressed some dissatisfaction with their own performance as Christians. They had failed to live up to the high ethical and moral standards that should be a part of the life of Christian discipleship.

But instead of agreeing with their self-debasement, Paul demonstrates the strategy of positive reinforcement, which so often succeeds where criticism fails.

In this Paul mirrors the method of Jesus himself. Anyone with half a mind could have discerned the sinfulness of the woman thrown like a dirty rag at Jesus' feet that day in the temple courtyard. Her critics accused her of adultery, and, indeed, she had been caught in the very act of it. But Jesus, after reminding the critics of their own faults, blessed the woman with the gentle assurance: "Neither do I condemn you" (John 8:10).

Everyone in Jericho knew what a swindler and liar Zacchaeus was. And when Jesus came face-to-face with this shrewd little politician, one would guess that the sparks would fly. What an easy mark Zacchaeus would be for Jesus' condemnation. Instead, when they met face-to-face, Jesus simply said, "Zacchaeus, hurry and come down; for I must stay at your house today" (Luke 19:5). Just a simple offer of friendship to one whose greed had left him friendless.

Paul ends this section of his letter with one of the most profoundly beautiful thoughts in the New Testament. Paul intimates that the glory of Christ is to be revealed in us ("so that the name of our Lord Jesus may be glorified in you"). We carry Christ's reputation around with us. Just as an artist's masterpiece is his greatest recommendation, so a Christian is proof of Christ's workmanship. We are his glory!

Can there be any greater privilege, or any greater responsibility than that?

DAY 100
Read 2 Thessalonians 2

A woman had been observed in church always bowing her head–as though in respect–whenever the name of the devil was mentioned. When questioned about this strange behavior, she replied, "Well, my dear, courtesy costs nothing, and one never knows where one might find oneself."

All people–Christians and non-Christians alike–have definite views of the devil. Some see the prince of darkness as a real persona–as real as Jesus. Some prefer to think of Satan as the personification of evil in the world, the face and name we have put on everything wicked. Still others feel that evil has no real identity in itself, that evil is simply the absence of good, just as cold is understood by scientists as being the absence of heat.

But no one can doubt the existence of evil in the world. And sometimes evil becomes terrifyingly personal. Martin Luther thought of the devil as such a real presence that he once threw an inkwell across the room to assault the satanic spirit he felt was present in the room.

And we all know how insidious the devil can be, in adopting disguises to deceive us. How clever the devil is, and how persistent! We may put the devil out of our minds from time to time, but we must be aware of the fact that the devil never stops thinking about us, or dreaming up ways to ensnare us. Though it may assault our modern sensitivities to give much thought to such a subject, we dare not assume that the devil has died, or we may one day discover to our horror that reports of his death, as Mark Twain would say, were greatly exaggerated.

Our only sure defense against the devil is God, who will ultimately triumph against all evil. Martin Luther included in his hymn "A Mighty Fortress Is Our God" the words:

And though this world, with devils filled, should threaten to undo us,
We will not fear, for God has willed his truth to triumph through us.
The prince of darkness grim, we tremble not for him;
His rage we can endure, for lo, his doom is sure.
One little word shall fell him.

And that one little word, spoken on reverent lips, is "God."

Surely there were times when Paul wished he could retrieve something that he had said. Hastily spoken words frequently come back to haunt us. But once a word is spoken, it is spoken; and nothing can make it be unspoken.

Such was the case with Paul's vivid teaching regarding Christ's second coming. "The day of the Lord will come like a thief in the night," he had warned the Thessalonian Christians in his first letter (5:2). And they had taken that warning to heart—so much so, in fact, that they had abandoned their work and ignored the daily responsibilities of life. If Christ was coming soon, they reasoned, it was useless to enter into contracts, or get married, or begin any new projects. Better to turn their backs on all earthly responsibilities and sit on some rooftop and await the cataclysmic event that would surely come within a few days.

So Paul wrote this second letter, in part, to warn them that even for a Christian who believes the Lord will come again there was work to be done and responsibilities to be fulfilled.

To provide an illustration of this teaching, Paul pointed out that he had not abandoned his work as a tentmaker. Everywhere Paul spent much time, he established his tent-making shop and began to take orders. And though no tents remain to provide proof of this belief, one must conclude that Paul was a competent worker, and fulfilled his obligations to his customers as fully and faithfully as he discharged his duties to his Lord.

It has been said of certain lazy Christians that "they are so heavenly-minded that they are no earthly good." And if that is true of some people, it is a betrayal of the Christian standard of life. Paul exhorts them, "Do [your] work quietly and earn [your] own living. Brothers and sisters, do not be weary in doing what is right."

A good citizen of the kingdom of heaven must also be a good citizen of the Earth. Before Jesus created salvation for all people, he first created yokes and tables for his customers in the carpenter's shop. And in both works he did his very best.

What do you think about, when you lie sleepless on your bed at three o'clock in the morning? Do you wonder what will happen to all those magnificent dreams that have been important to you, and that you have spent your life trying to translate into deed? Do you wonder if anybody will carry on the work that you have begun, or if the world will simply leave your unfinished work unfinished, gradually to be reclaimed by the jungle? Do you wonder if those truths that you have spent your life expressing and supporting will no longer be spoken, when you are no longer around to speak them? Will anybody know you've been here, and will anybody care?

Those were questions that surely filled Paul's mind, as he spent each day from his dwindling reservoir of them, in prison in Rome. He had been a faithful and vigorous missionary and apologist for the Christian faith. Dozens of congregations existed because of his ministry, and the number of converts he had brought to Christ would be uncountable. But even with his magnificent accomplishments, a sea of weaknesses within and heresies without threatened to erode the church. What would happen when Paul was no longer alive to lead the church against its foes?

Perhaps it was with those concerns in mind that Paul began, early in his ministry, to enlist young leaders to learn from him, and later to assume his responsibilities, like Mark and Titus. But probably the name that leaps first to mind is Timothy. A native of Lystra, the son of a Jewish mother and a Greek father, Timothy came under Paul's influence when the apostle visited Timothy's hometown on his second missionary journey. Having lost his first young apprentice when Mark abandoned him on his previous missionary journey, Paul asked Timothy to join the team. And thus began a ministry that was to have remarkable consequences.

Timothy was now Paul's handpicked successor as minister of the church at Ephesus. And Paul wrote his two letters to Timothy to assure that the young minister's theology was accurate, and that his administrative skills would effectively lead the church he served. So two New Testament books were written by an old apostle to a young minister, to make sure Paul's dream did not end when his life did.

However few and poor your material possessions might be, you will surely make some arrangements to ensure that they are appropriately transferred when you are gone. But isn't your Christian faith worth more to you than houses and lands?

What are you doing to guarantee that the truths you cherish and the church you have served with your life will continue to prosper when you are gone?

Paul's teaching about women in the church has been subjected to two tragedies: a misunderstanding of the local circumstances in which Paul's words made sense, and inappropriate application in local circumstances in which Paul's words make no sense.

Before we can begin to understand how we are to interpret these teachings, we must give some thought to the situation in which they were written.

There were two cultures existing side by side in Ephesus. One was the Greek culture. As one of the largest and most sophisticated cities of the Greek world, Ephesus was thoroughly suffused with the religion of the pagan gods. One of the city's proudest landmarks was the temple of Artemis (or Diana), also remembered as one of the seven wonders of the ancient world. Not only were most of the residents thoroughly Greek in their religious practices, the city also attracted a large number of pilgrims each year, to visit the world-renowned temple.

In its worship practices, women had only one role: as "priestesses" whose one duty was to satisfy the lust of the men who came to visit the temple. Respectable women in Ephesus remained in constant seclusion, to avoid being mistaken for these "holy prostitutes."

There was also a large population of Jewish people who had come to Ephesus to escape the "ethnic cleansing" efforts of the Roman army of occupation in Jerusalem. Despite the extreme differences between the Greek and the Jewish Ephesians, they shared one common belief: that no respectable woman would be seen in public, and never in a position of leadership.

It was to avoid the reputation that the church was a company of loose and immoral women that Paul bowed to the mores of that time and place. One must choose one's battles carefully, and perhaps the apostle felt that this was one battle that would be too costly.

But there can be no question that the Christian faith brought a new life of freedom and respect to women. The church was immeasurably blessed by the leadership of such women as Phoebe, Priscilla, and all those women whose names are reverently listed by Paul in the sixteenth chapter of Romans. And though Paul might say to the Ephesians (as Jesus said to his disciples), "I still have many things to say to you, but you cannot bear them now" (John 16:12), he would find the courage to say it plainly at other times: "There is no longer Jew or Greek, there is no longer slave or free, there is no longer male and female; for all of you are one in Christ Jesus" (Galatians 3:28).

It is clear that by the time Paul wrote this letter to Timothy, the church had developed an organizational structure to facilitate its work. People who abhor organization in the church because, as they claim, "it's unscriptural" have forgotten that Jesus organized his followers into a group of apostles, with at least one office (treasurer). And when he accomplished that miracle of feeding a multitude of people with the contents of one boy's lunch bucket, he organized the crowd into companies of fifty, to facilitate the serving.

The church had not been in existence very long before it was discovered that deacons were needed, to assure that the benevolent ministries of the church were distributed equitably (Acts 6:1–6). And though we are not given information about the exact time or circumstances when the church recognized its need of elders, it is obvious that such had been the case.

The church had inherited from its Jewish ancestry the concept of the eldership—a tradition that reached back into their history all the way to Moses. As the sole leader of a large and contentious nation, trying to survive in the wilderness of Sinai, Moses accepted the idea presented to him by his father-in-law (Numbers 11), and appointed seventy men who would share the rigors of leadership with Moses. By the time of Jesus' ministry, the seventy elders had become the Sanhedrin.

But it was obvious to the few seasoned and commissioned leaders like Paul and Peter that each congregation needed people with special gifts and unquestioned integrity who would provide direction and guidance to the flock.

The leadership to be provided by the elders and deacons should be of two kinds: they would lead by precept (teaching) and by example. In fact, Paul has far more to say to Timothy about the character requirements than the skills such leaders would need.

The pastor of a small church was complaining about the lack of qualified leadership in the church. He said, "The good ain't able, and the able ain't good." But leaders in the church must be both good and able. And there is some role of leadership—however modest—for every Christian. God has called us to that ministry. And we must "bloom where we are planted."

Some of the troublemakers about whom Paul warned Timothy were Gnostics. Although their philosophy cannot be expressed in a few words, one of the major beliefs of Gnosticism was that all spirit is good and all matter is evil, and that never the twain would meet. They did not believe that Jesus could possibly be both human and divine, so they opted to believe that he was strictly and simply divine—that he was not subject to the needs of the body (like hunger for food), and that he could never experience weariness or sorrow.

So the Gnostics tried to persuade the Christians at Ephesus that the only way they could live a life that would please God would be to eschew all reliance upon physical resources. They believed that food was evil and should be avoided except for a small amount to stave off starvation. And they believed that those extreme aesthetes who starved themselves to death were destined for sainthood.

They likewise believed that marriage was evil, and that labor in the world was blasphemy. The influence of this false teaching made its impact on some branches of the church in the Middle Ages, in which monks and nuns went without food, declined to marry, and abandoned the work of the world for the sake of their religion. Some even moved to the desert, to remove themselves, as much as was humanly possible, from all earthly delights.

But Jesus proved, by his immense enjoyment of human companionship and his provision of food for hungry people, that he accepted the joys of the world as gifts from God. He obviously believed that everything God made was good.

But there are people who believe that self-deprivation is a goal of the Christian life, and the more we rob ourselves of happiness, the more we please God. Paul, however, insists that we do not serve God by enslaving ourselves with strict rules and regulations, and denigrating God's creation. Rather, we serve God by gratefully accepting God's good gifts and remembering that we live in a world in which God made all things well, and by remembering to share those good gifts with others.

"God setteth the solitary in families." So the *King James Version* translates Psalm 68:6. The *New Revised Standard Version* renders it, "God gives the desolate a home to live in." Though arguments could be put forth to defend the greater accuracy of either, the essential truth is that the human family is God's plan, and that each of us was given the experience of family as a human legacy. And while not all human families fulfill the holy intention, most of us can claim some experience upon which to base our understanding of this verse of scripture.

So we can understand Paul's instructions to Timothy regarding the most helpful attitude he might show toward other people, by putting it in familial terms. Thus, the young minister was to conduct himself toward an older man as if the man were his father. Younger men should be regarded as brothers. Older women should be treated as mothers, and younger women as sisters. The family provided the template by which all human relationships in the church were to be carved.

In the church—as in the family—we accept one another. In his poem "Death of the Hired Man" Robert Frost said, "Home is where, when you have to go there, they have to take you in." And so in the church: Whatever their race, whatever their economic status, whatever their personality traits, those who come to Christ and his church are to be accepted as brothers and sisters.

And we must bear one another's burdens, and seek to fulfill each other's needs in the church. And we do so without reluctance or complaint. "He ain't heavy, mister, he's my brother" is the rule. Or maybe he is heavy, and maybe he is disgusting, and maybe he costs us plenty, but if he is a brother, we will carry him anyway.

And in the family we forgive each other, even as Christ has forgiven us. And we inspire each other. And, above all, we love each other. Like all brothers and sisters we may have differences and complaints, but at the end of the day, we know who our brothers and sisters are, and it shows in how we conduct ourselves at home.

Here, in this sixth chapter of First Timothy is a warning that is probably even more timely and appropriate now than when it was written. "Those who want to be rich fall into temptation," Paul says (v. 9). And who of us does not want to be rich? A sardonic bumper sticker says, "I've been rich and I've been poor, and believe me, rich is better." A popular television program asks the rhetorical question, "Who wants to be a millionaire?" Although the inborn instinct for self-preservation calls for a certain amount of security, most of us do not know when to say, "I have enough."

A Roman proverb asserted that wealth is like seawater: rather than quenching our thirst, the more one drinks of it, the more he wants to drink.

From beginning to end the Bible cautions against materialism, which is simply an expression of distrust in God. "Strive first for the kingdom of God and his righteousness, and all these things will be given to you as well"(Matthew 6:33). But our problem with God's providence is that the divine plan promises us only "daily bread," when we prefer to have one loaf in the bread box, two more in the kitchen cabinet, several more in the freezer, and enough "bread" in the bank to buy enough loaves in the future for a mountain of sandwiches.

Paul warns, "the love of money is a root of all kinds of evil" (v. 10). Note that the common vernacular translates it "money is the root of all evil." And although that is close, it is inaccurate enough to make the saying untrue. Money is not "the" root of "all evil," but "a root" of "all kinds of evil." To be sure, there are other roots that produce evil branches: lust, pride, and deceit, to name a few. But no human fault is more insidious than materialism, because it puts money on the throne that properly belongs to God.

But Paul hastens to assure us that our Christian faith need not deprive us of such material resources as life needs, in order for happiness to be possible. "God richly provides us with everything for our enjoyment" (v. 17). But Paul also warns us that we must be generous in sharing the good things God has given us. God gives to us so that we might have something to give to others.

Contentment is not to be found in having what we want, but in wanting what we have.

DAY 108
Read 2 Timothy 1

The Greek word *paratheke* was essentially a business word that meant "deposit." It described the transaction when a person surrenders his money to a bank in the faith that the bank will keep it safe and return it to him upon demand.

Let that meaning of the word *paratheke* stay in your mind as you recall that when he was dying on the cross Jesus said, "Father, into thy hands I *paratheke* my spirit." Jesus was depositing his spirit in hands that were strong and secure, hands that would keep him through all the rigors of death, and would return his life to him at the other end of that ordeal.

It was that same word that Paul utilized in his saying to Timothy, "I am not ashamed, for I know the one in whom I have put my trust, and I am sure that he is able to guard until that day what I have *paratheke*-ed to him" (v. 12). Sick, old, in prison, facing the daily possibility of execution, Paul nevertheless had found a safe and secure "safe deposit box" into which he had placed his hopes for the future, and his record of service on behalf of the gospel.

This magnificent confidence was made possible because of Paul's faith. He had something better than blind trust upon which to base his hope. It was the certain knowledge that had resulted from decades of trusting God and discovering, in every experience, that God was as good as his word. "I know," Paul said. And what he knew for sure was not a theology nor a system of rituals and rules, but a person: "I know the one in whom I have put my trust."

Fanny Crosby, the sightless hymn-writer of the last century, was once called upon by Phoebe Knapp, the wife of the president of Metropolitan Life Insurance Company. After they had shared their faith with each other, the guest started to leave, but being true to her husband's life work, she asked Miss Crosby if she had adequate life insurance. "I don't need insurance," she replied, "because I have a Blessed Assurance–that Jesus is mine." And thus was born one of America's favorite hymns.

And that was the assurance that gave Paul confidence as he faced a difficult present and an uncertain future.

DAY 109
Read 2 Timothy 2

Reading between the lines, we must conclude that Timothy had faced some severe difficulties in his ministry, and may have been tempted to let his sufferings turn him aside from his loyal service. It is ironic that service to Christ should result in suffering, but the fact is that suffering is an unavoidable element in every life. Neither the Christian nor the atheist can avoid it. "Human beings are born to trouble," Job concluded, "just as sparks fly upward" (Job 5:7). And while every Christian may expect trouble in his or her life, it is possible for us to find some glory in our suffering.

A woman who was troubled with chronic insomnia finally, after many years of suffering this difficulty, found a way to endure it with patience and meaning. She remembered that when Jesus was suffering his ordeal in the Garden of Gethsemane, he expressed disappointment that his disciples—his closest friends—were peacefully sleeping. "Could you not stay awake with me one hour?" he asked (Matthew 26:40). He asked so little for himself, and was facing such a severe test, and one can surely understand his desire to have someone share his anguish. So the sleepless woman turned her anxiety over her insomnia into an intentional time of drawing closer to her Lord.

Like any experience in life, suffering can be a bane or a blessing. Labor pains can produce new life. An athlete's rigorous expenditure of effort can result in physical fitness and victory on the playing field. And a soldier's willingness to endure hardship and pain can lead to the kind of faithfulness that wins a battle.

But suffering may also rob us of our faith and embitter our outlook. Each of us has the right to choose whether our troubles make us bitter or better.

Most people prefer sunshine to clouds and rain. But all sunshine would produce a desert. And while we may learn something from pleasure and ease, it is from tragedy and grief that we learn the most. The Christian faith has splendid credentials as a means of gaining victories in the midst of defeat, for its founder won Earth's greatest triumph on a cross of agony.

DAY 110

In seeking to understand this reading, one is stopped cold by Paul's reference to "Jannes and Jambres," who are identified simply as two men who opposed Moses, and who were "of corrupt mind and counterfeit faith" (v. 8). Who, we want to know, were these two? A search of the books of Moses turns up no mention of their names, nor does any other portion of the Bible. But a little investigation clears up the mystery. To find the solution we must know something about the Talmud—the body of Hebrew traditions, rituals, rules, and teachings of the elders, which did not make their way into the canon of the Old Testament.

According to this Talmud, Jannes and Jambres were Pharaoh's court magicians, referred to in Exodus 7. When Moses came to call on Pharaoh to demand the release of the Hebrew slaves, he had certain tricks up his sleeve. At God's instruction, Moses cast down his rod and it became a serpent. But Pharaoh's magicians were able to duplicate this trick by their own magic.

Moses further demonstrated the divine power at work through him by accomplishing various other remarkable deeds. Each time Jannes and Jambres duplicated the feat. But although the works of the magicians were spectacular, their sensational effects were only cosmetic. After the applause died down, there was nothing left. But the power of God in Moses was able to redeem a whole nation of people, and lead them through a forty-year odyssey in the desert, and bring them, at last, to a new land.

In every age sensationalism has attracted its devotees. Whatever puts on the flashiest show and makes the most noise is frequently mistaken for authentic religion. But the real test of genuine religion is not how it looks or sounds, but what it results in, in the lives of people. Is anybody released from any bondage through its power? Is anybody prompted to live sacrificially and magnanimously because of it? Does it champion anybody's human rights, or protect anybody's honor, or lift up any broken hearts or mend anybody's broken dreams? If that's what you want from your religion, don't call on Jannes and Jambres, but on the God of Moses.

After a long and astonishingly successful career as a missionary, Paul was facing the end of his life, living out his last days in a prison cell in Rome. There, despite his age, infirmity, and near-blindness, Paul wrote seven of the books of the New Testament, including this second letter to his young minister-protégé, Timothy. In fact, it is entirely possible that this letter—so full of affection and inspiration—was the last letter Paul ever wrote.

But in addition to the weightier matters to be dealt with, the old apostle had a few personal requests. Chief among them was Paul's request that Timothy might come to see him. It is only natural that Paul wanted to have one last visit with this young man, whom Paul loved like the son he never had. But one must be deeply touched by the inclusion of some small, seemingly insignificant details in Paul's urging that Timothy come to him. He said, "When you come, bring the cloak that I left...at Troas." It was summer when Paul was at Troas, and the warm cloak was excess baggage. But now that winter was coming on, Paul faced the real prospect of suffering from the cold. He didn't need a new cloak, and he wasn't asking for a charitable gift. All he was asking for was the return of an old cloak that would give him a modicum of comfort in a cold and damp prison cell, in the evening of his life.

Toward the end of this chapter, Paul renewed his request to Timothy, pleading, "Do your best to come before winter" (v. 21). Why before winter? Because when winter set in, the season for navigation in the Mediterranean was at an end. If Timothy did not come before winter, he would have to wait until spring. And Paul had the premonition that "the time of my departure has come" (v. 6). So if Timothy was to come at all, it had to be "before winter."

Life is too short and time is too fleeting for us to deny ourselves the most priceless treasures, which we may purchase only with the time God lends us day by day. We're too much in a hurry to get through time, just to arrive at some future date when we think life will really begin. So we treat our days as though they were disposable tissues—use up this one, "and up pops another one." But when will we learn that there is not an inexhaustible supply of days, and that in every day there are some opportunities that may never be ours again?

DAY 112
Read Titus 1

In a youth Sunday school class the students were discussing the biblical story of David and Goliath. The teacher asked the pupils to reflect on this question: "How was David able to conquer the giant when none of the soldiers of Israel could?" After a moment's reflection one student said, "I think it was because of their attitude. All the soldiers looked at Goliath and said, 'How can I possibly defeat him?' But David looked at the giant and said, 'He's so big, how can I possibly miss him?'"

Such was surely the optimistic confidence Paul had about the island of Crete when he left the young minister Titus to be the pastor of the new church there.

Even among the scandalous reputations of the other places in the Aegean world, Crete enjoyed a sinister and unenviable notoriety. Wherever in ancient Greek literature Crete is mentioned, it is always as an insult. It was prejudicial then, and it still is, to lump all people of a certain racial or ethnic group into a derogatory designation. "Racial profiling" is always a lie, because it assumes that everyone of a certain racial stock shares the same proclivities. What on earth, then, was Paul doing indulging in such a vicious insult by claiming, "Cretans are always liars, vicious brutes, lazy gluttons" (v. 12)? Talk about politically incorrect! Surely someone from the Anti-Defamation League should pay a visit to Paul!

But note that Paul does not say, "Such people are hopeless—have nothing to do with them." Rather, he said, in effect, "See what the world says about these people. Let them become examples of how Christ can redeem even the most unrighteous life."

Furthermore, the reading indicates that not only had congregations been planted in that hopelessly infertile soil, sufficient growth had taken place that elders had been appointed. And the list of virtues that Paul indicates are qualifications for eldership suggests that the Cretan elders were at least as conscientious and faithful as the average elders in today's church.

The fact is, Crete presented a "before and after" picture of what happens to a person when Christ enters his life. And with such proof, who of us can fear that we are not good enough to be Christian, or to be a member of the church? Such a question is always quite beside the point, because the power that makes us Christian is not how good we are, but how good our Christ is.

Each of us is born into an imperfect world, to live in a faulty society composed of defective people. Our reaction to this unfortunate reality must take one of two courses: First, we may be like the cynics, the school of Greek philosophers who believed that no one and nothing was good, that everything and everybody was hopelessly and irreparably evil. Probably the best-remembered cynic was Diogenes, who, it is said, went about with a lighted lantern, looking in vain for one honest man.

But there is another choice: We can accept the world as it is, and recognize what is good in it and celebrate that, and acknowledge what is bad, and correct it if we can. But if we can't, we mustn't expend all our strength and resources seeking to change an unalterable wrong. Reinhold Niebuhr expressed this latter course when he taught us to pray:

Lord, grant me the serenity to accept what I cannot change,
The courage to change what I can,
And the wisdom to know the difference.

Some Bible scholars have taken Paul to task for not condemning slavery and actively working toward the overthrow of that evil. But as monumental as Paul's contributions to society were, he was limited by the ruling structure in which he lived.

But Paul did something better than change a faulty system: he changed the people within that system until the system no longer had the power to dehumanize and degrade people.

So Paul urges Titus to "tell slaves to be submissive to their masters, and to give satisfaction in every respect" (v. 9). But remember that Paul also had instructed the slave-masters, "Do the same to them" (that is, to slaves) (Ephesians 6:9). What Paul did was to create a new system of human relationships that transcended earthly stations. Such an ideal was expressed in Paul's letter to Philemon, in which he begged that Christian master to receive his runaway slave, Onesimus, not as a slave, but as a Christian brother.

As in dealing with all laws and rules, "The written code kills, but the Spirit gives life" (2 Corinthians 3:6). Let your relationships be determined not by any written code, but by the spirit of Christ within you.

There is a striking paradox here, which lies at the very heart of the Christian life. Paul labors—here as elsewhere—to assure his readers that our salvation does not result from good works we have done. "He saved us, not because of any works of righteousness that we had done, but according to his mercy" (v. 5). But once that glorious truth has been established, Paul urges, "that those who have come to believe in God may be careful to devote themselves to good works" (v. 8). So, then: Are good works an essential part of Christian discipleship or not?

The answer, of course, is an unequivocal "yes and no." "No," because all the good works in the world could never earn salvation for us, but "Yes, " because if we have really received God's grace, we should be so filled with gratitude that no one can keep us from expressing that gratitude in a life that reflects divine grace in our human generosity.

Love has a motive power far greater than that of fear or greed or hatred. And love makes demands upon us that no rules or laws could enforce. "The love of Christ urges us on," the apostle said (2 Corinthians 5:14).

Even in its adolescent expressions, love makes claims upon us that rules are powerless to enforce. Picture a teenage boy who has studiously avoided the bathtub as though afraid he might dissolve in it, and whose grooming and dress have made his parents hope the dog catcher does not see him. When he suddenly begins devoting hours to his appearance, and his presence can be detected half a mile away by some heavenly fragrance, it may safely be concluded that love has entered the picture. What his parents failed to make him do out of obedience to rules, he gladly does in response to love.

Isaac Watts expressed the constraint of Christ's self-sacrificing love for us in the words of his hymn "When I Survey the Wondrous Cross":

> Were the whole realm of nature mine,
> That were a present far too small;
> Love so amazing, so divine
> Demands my soul, my life, my all.

And such demands lead us to do, joyfully and gladly, what obedience to rules could never achieve.

DAY 115
Read Philemon

Though one of the briefest books in the Bible, the charming letter of Paul to Philemon is surely one of the most inspiring. Unfortunately, the story that may be drawn from it ends in a most intriguing cliffhanger. Paul had sent a runaway slave, Onesimus, back to his owner, Philemon, with a letter that urged the master to forgive the slave, and to receive him as a Christian brother. Did Philemon accede to Paul's urging and accept his runaway slave as a brother? Unfortunately, the Bible offers us no clue. But a bit of history may provide the answer to our puzzle.

History tells of a great Christian leader, the bishop of Ephesus, who, having been a friend and coworker with Paul at some time, assumed after Paul's death the work of collecting, editing, and publishing the epistles of Paul, putting them in the form in which they appear in our Bible. And the name of that towering Christian leader was Onesimus—so unusual a name, even in that day, that it is far easier to believe that it was the same Onesimus who began his Christian life as a slave, shared Paul's prison cell where he served as Paul's secretary, and, released from bondage by his Christian master, grew into a position of respected leadership in the church, than to believe that there were two men with the same unusual name who figured prominently in the history of the early church.

As Philemon stood looking at his returned slave and read the letter from Paul beseeching him to let his Christian faith dictate his decision, surely he could not have guessed how far-reaching his decision would be. How could he know that the Christian standing before him would provide dedicated leadership to the whole Christian movement in Asia Minor, and that nineteen centuries later, hundreds of millions of Christians all around the world would still reap the fruits of his labors as they find inspiration in the letters of Paul that Onesimus collected, edited, preserved, and published? What if Philemon had failed?

And what are the tragic results when we fail to let the love of Christ within us determine our willingness to receive any of Christ's followers as our brothers and sisters? As an old Scotsman said, "If you forget who you are durin' the day, how'll you know where to come in at evenin'?"

Much of the Epistle to the Hebrews is shrouded in mystery. We have no clue to its author or to the congregation or congregations to which it was written. One thing is certain, however: This epistle sought to remind Christians of Jewish background that Christianity was not a repudiation of Judaism, but a fulfillment of it.

The letter begins by affirming the glorious truth that God seeks us through many doors and a variety of means. God is able to speak through any language or circumstance that fits our hearing. "In many and various ways," God proclaimed the holy truth through the prophets. And every prophet had a piece of the truth that God had inspired. Amos had called for social justice. Jonah had appealed for the acceptance of outsiders, in the belief that all people were God's people. Hosea had insisted that mercy toward the sinful was more God-like than judgment and condemnation. And while each spoke the truth, it was only a partial truth.

An old poem imagines a scene in which several blind men try to perceive what an elephant is like, though each sightless man is limited in his perception to what he can discover, by feeling with his outstretched hand, that part of the elephant that falls within his range.

As an elephant is so much greater than any one person's grasp, so God is infinitely superior to any one prophet's understanding.

But when Jesus came, he revealed all the magnificent fullness of God. Like Amos, Jesus cared about those unjustly dealt with, and championed their cause. Like Jonah, Jesus cared about all people, regardless of their ethnicity or moral uprightness. Like Hosea, Jesus demonstrated an astonishing acceptance and forgiveness of even the most sinful.

So Jesus was "the reflection of God's glory." Does that mean, then, that we are to ignore the prophets who, in centuries past, spoke God's word? Not at all! But only in Christ is the fullness of God pleased to dwell. And the prophets, as useful as they were in bringing to people a glimpse of God's glory, were only "previews of coming attractions" that would be revealed in Christ.

The truth to be learned from all this is that everyone is given a piece of the glory of God. And as fragmentary as our knowledge might be, it is our responsibility to cherish the best that we know, and do our best to live by it.

It is not surprising that the writer should include a reference to a Psalm. What is surprising is that either the writer did not remember, or for some reason chose not to identify, the source of the reference. "Someone has testified somewhere..." We must remember that even the most devout Christians did not have ready access to a copy of the scriptures, as we do. So when an appropriate scripture text occurred to the writer, he could not quickly search the scriptures to find the source.

Fortunately, we do have access to the Bible, though we frequently forget that such a precious blessing, which has become common to us, would have been considered a spiritual luxury of great importance to people of other ages. An old saying reminds us, "Those who do not read have no real advantage over those who cannot read." And that is true of our failure to avail ourselves of our easy access to the Bible.

But without doubt the saying that is referred to here is the eighth Psalm: "What are human beings that you are mindful of them, or mortals, that you care for them? You have made them for a little while lower than the angels." That is an accurate recording of the Greek translation of the psalm. But even more astonishing is the accurate translation of the original Hebrew of that passage, which states, surprisingly, "You have made them a little lower than God."

What a declaration of the divinely intended stature of human beings! As the psalm continues, "You have given them dominion over the works of your hands, and have put all things under their feet" (Psalm 8:6). God has made us second in command to the authority of the Creator of all things. God intended us to be the apex of creation, the heir of divine glory, the partner with the divine in the fulfillment of earth's purpose.

But the writer of Hebrews continues by lamenting that we have failed to live up to that divine intention. We, who were intended by the Creator to be free, have allowed ourselves to be imprisoned by sin, our divine prerogatives surrendered to our human weaknesses. But into this tragedy comes Jesus Christ, one of us yet the perfect representation of God, who through his sacrifice has restored the glory meant to be our destiny.

No matter what you are or how you have failed, Jesus Christ can rescue your birthright and restore you to the radiance God wants to share with the children of the Supreme Being.

In arguing for the supreme uniqueness of Jesus Christ, the writer first showed how Jesus was superior to the prophets. His next step was to argue that Jesus occupied a higher position than the angels. Finally, he argues that Jesus was greater than Moses. This may seem, at first, an anticlimax, but we must remember that to the Jews, Moses was the very embodiment of the Hebrew faith. It was Moses who rescued the whole nation from their bondage in Egypt, and led them through forty days of sojourn in the wilderness, and brought them to the very border of their promised land. And most of all, it was Moses through whom God gave the Law upon which the faith of Israel was based. If ever a human being could be said to be a faithful servant of God, it was Moses.

But faithful though he was, he was inevitably a servant, whereas Jesus was a son and heir. Furthermore, Jesus was both an apostle and a high priest. Elsewhere in the New Testament the word "apostle" is used to refer to those who were a part of Jesus' company of coworkers, as well as to Paul himself. But the writer of this letter reserves the title for Jesus alone. He was the one whom God sent (*apostolos* means "the sent one.") An ambassador is one who is given the authority to represent and to speak on behalf of the country that sends him. So Jesus was sent here by God with all the authority to represent God and to speak on God's behalf.

But Jesus had another identity, which Moses could not claim: he was high priest. The Latin word for priest is *pontifex,* which means "bridge-builder." Jesus came to build a bridge between heaven and earth, between sinful human beings and the righteous God. "In Christ God was reconciling the world to himself," Paul wrote (2 Corinthians 5:19).

It is said that when King Edward VIII of England abdicated his throne to marry Wallis Simpson, the entire world was listening to the live radio transmission of his address. But in an American radio station a crucial wire broke, interrupting the broadcast. An engineer at the station quickly picked up both of the broken ends and the signal passed through his body, to complete the circuit. It was a heroic thing to do, and it resulted in his death. But Europe and America were brought together through the selfless sacrifice of one man.

So heaven and earth were brought together through Christ's selfless sacrifice. Though it cost him his life, he brought God and God's alienated family together.

After laboring the point of Jesus' divine supremacy, the writer of the Epistle to the Hebrews makes an abrupt change and shows us a Jesus who shares with us every human trait and temptation: "For we do not have a high priest who is unable to sympathize with our weaknesses, but we have one who in every respect has been tempted as we are" (v. 15).

A frequently heard phrase these days is "been there, done that." Sometimes it expresses boredom or condescension toward another's recitation of a trouble. But often the phrase denotes empathy and concern. "You are having difficulty making ends meet? Been there, done that! You say the demands of your work leave little time for rest and recreation? Been there, done that! Your grown children don't have any time for you, unless they need something? Been there, done that!"

To be sure, there are times when the attitude behind that familiar phrase is the reverse of "one-upmanship" (or "one-downmanship" perhaps?). Whatever your problems are, mine are greater. Whatever difficult patch of life you are going through, I was there 'way ahead of you. Such an attitude is an unfortunate amalgamation of self-pity and self-aggrandizement.

But when the phrase is said in sincere concern and sympathy, it can be enormously comforting. "I know what you are going through, because I've been there, too, and I understand and care."

So Jesus makes the perfect high priest, for although he was without sin, he faced every kind of temptation we face. And despite his ultimate triumph, he experienced every kind of weakness that plagues us. If we grieve over the death of loved ones, we can remember that Jesus wept at the tomb of Lazarus. If we sometimes wonder if the heavens are empty and deaf to our prayers, we can think of Jesus in the Garden of Gethsemane, sending up to God a desperate plea that seemed to return to him marked "addressee unknown." If panic grips your throat like an unknown assailant whenever you think of the inevitability of death, remember that Jesus did not want to die, either. If you sometimes feel that your friends have forsaken you, think of Jesus standing before Pontius Pilate, with no friendly face in that multitude shouting, "Crucify!"

Whatever weakness or sorrow or temptation you face, Jesus has "been there, done that." And because he understands what you are facing, he knows exactly what help to give you in your time of trial. Can you find victory even in such hopeless circumstances as you now face? "Yes!" Jesus assures you. "I know you can, because I've been there and done that!"

DAY 120
Read Hebrews 5

In laboring to make the concept of the priesthood of Christ understandable to his readers, the writer of Hebrews lamented that his readers, even after many years of experience as Christians, were still in the kindergarten of their faith. They were content to remain toddlers in rompers when they should be developing a maturity that would not continue to clamor for simplifications and elementary concepts.

Somehow it has become a common belief that the concepts that compose the Christian gospel ought to be reducible to a few basic and easily understood maxims.

A noted theologian was sitting beside another man on a long airplane flight. Their conversation revealed that the man seated beside the theologian was an astronomer. When the astronomer learned that his seat-mate was a theologian, he said, "Well, I guess you might say I'm a theologian, too; and my theology is 'live and let live.'" The theologian replied, "Well, I guess you might say I'm an astronomer, as well. And my astronomy is 'twinkle, twinkle, little star.'"

But if, as we claim, the Christian faith is the most magnificent set of beliefs and values ever revealed to human beings, and if we trust this religion to deliver us from all our human weaknesses and dangers, including death, surely we ought to be able to spend some time and effort to gain some intellectual and spiritual maturity in so supremely important a matter. Indeed, a bit earlier in this letter, the writer warned, "How can we escape if we neglect so great a salvation?" (Hebrews 2:3).

A cautionary tale once current in preparatory school classes told of a girl whose teacher assigned her to write a one-thousand-word theme. She labored over that assignment, and when it was complete, it represented her best work, and the teacher rewarded her with an A. The next year she received a similar assignment, and since she had a different teacher, she turned in the theme she had written before. It was the very same theme, but this year it was given a B. She tried the deception again the next year, and was shocked to receive a failing grade.

The Christian life ought to be a life of growth and learning, and should result in deeper commitment, increasing generosity, enlarging visions, and ever more intimate companionship with God. And the last day of your life should be your best, and when you have lived that last day, you should be only one short step into the presence of God.

DAY 121
Read Hebrews 6

In Henryk Sienkiewicz's novel *Quo Vadis,* the closing scene is pregnant with meaning. The author pictures Peter toward the end of his ministry. He has been a strong and vigorous leader for the persecuted Christians in the pagan city of Rome. His courage and dedication have won splendid victories for the kingdom of God. But now he is an old soldier, bent with his burden of years. At the urging of his friends he is leaving the city of Rome, retiring from the arena of combat, yielding to others the defense of the church against Caesar's latest threats of persecution.

At the edge of the city, Peter pauses a moment. The quiet, serene countryside beckons him, promising leisure and rest, and the tranquil evening of life, with its cherished companions. Then he is startled to see a vision of the Christ. But the Lord does not pause, as Peter is pausing, but seems intent on his journey. Peter calls to him, "Quo vadis, Domine?" ("Where are you going, Lord?") And the Christ answers him, "If you desert me, then I must go back to the city to be crucified again."

And Peter, the old soldier of the cross, straightens up, his burden of weariness and age no longer heavy, and follows his Master back to the city.

Although this presumption cannot be verified in records, one must assume that Sienkiewicz surely found the inspiration for his story in the passage from Hebrews in which the writer warns his readers of the shocking consequences of falling away from their Christian discipleship. "They are crucifying again the Son of God," the writer warns (v. 6).

The horrifying moment in history when Christ hung on the cross is but a glimpse of what God always is and always does. If the sins of a certain group of people living at a particular time and place resulted in divine agony and sorrow, then that is what happens in this time and place when we betray our God.

When Rembrandt completed his stirring painting of the crucifixion, his friends were shocked, as they examined the painting, that the artist had included a "cameo" appearance of himself in the scene—not as one of Jesus' faithful friends (for Rembrandt was a Christian) but as one of the ugly mob, his face contorted in hatred as he joined the chorus of voices demanding, "Crucify him."

If the first Good Friday should come again, and your life cast the deciding vote, would Christ be crucified again?

Melchizedek is one of the most mysterious characters in the entire Bible. All we know about him from the Old Testament is contained in two very short passages. In one of them (Psalm 110:4) there is only a brief statement that the coming Messiah would be "a priest forever, according to the order of Melchizedek."

The only portion of scripture that tells us anything about this shadowy character is in the fourteenth chapter of Genesis. Melchizedek is identified as the "King of Salem" (which would later become Jerusalem), and this priest, whose ancestry was completely unknown, blessed Abram and gave him bread and wine, and Abram presented tithes of all that he possessed to this priest. The name "Melchizedek" means "King of Righteousness."

What can we say about this mysterious character that will help us to understand why the writer of Hebrews uses it to explain Christ's authority and ministry?

First, Melchizedek was not appointed by men, but by God. God always provides an access to heaven, some bridge over which human beings can pass in order to gain entrance to God's eternal kingdom. And the function of the priest is to be a bridge-builder. And in the dawn of time, before churches and seminaries and theologians and preachers, God raised up one who would be present and available when someone—like Abraham—was looking for the path to God.

The children of a kindergarten class had been asked to share with the class information about the work done by their fathers. One child proudly announced, "My daddy is a doctor." Another announced, "My daddy is a truck driver." But if there had been a prize in that competition, it would surely have gone to the lad who pointed proudly to the man sitting in the back row and said, "My daddy is *here!*" As far as the boy was concerned, it was "being here" that was the major work of his parent.

And that is the major work of Jesus Christ—our high priest. When we feel the need to turn to God, for forgiveness or encouragement or guidance or comfort or any other need, God is *here*—because of our high priest.

One major difference between the religion of the Hebrews and the Christian faith is that the Old Testament faith began with a written word: the tablets of stone on which the Ten Commandments were written. Subsequent teachings were established and perpetuated through the writings of the prophets and the teachers of the faith. The Word was accepted as the sign and seal of God's outreaching concern for the people of Israel.

When the Word became flesh in the incarnation, there was surprisingly little written documentation of that magnificent event and its meaning for human beings. The gospel was a "word of mouth" tradition for several years after the church began. Possibly it was because the early Christian leaders were convinced that Christ's imminent return to earth would make such written transcripts moot. Or it may have been simply that the new gospel was such incredibly good news that the excitement of those who heard it wouldn't allow them to sit still long enough to compose carefully worded documents to communicate it. It was not until the second generation of the church, when eyewitnesses to Christ's ministry could no longer give their firsthand accounts, that the letters of Paul and others began to reduce to the written word what had been primarily an oral tradition.

In any case, unlike its Jewish antecedent, the Christian faith was not a system of rules and laws that required written codification, but was a matter of experience and understandings acquired through intimate associations with the living Christ. When Paul said, "I know" (as he frequently did) he was expressing a conviction that had not been learned in a library, but proven in faith.

Perhaps that was God's intention in the first place, for as the writer of the Hebrew epistle recalled from the writings of Jeremiah, God says, "This is the covenant that I will make with the house of Israel...I will put my laws in their minds and write them on their hearts, and I will be their God" (v. 10). If the spirit of Christ abides in you, then your own mind becomes the rulebook and your own heart sets the standards for your life. You need no written word to tell you what is right and wrong, or what God would want you to do. Just think with your Christ-cleansed mind and feel with the new heart that the Redeemer has set to beating within your chest. That may seem rather vague to those who do not know our Christ, but as the poet said:

...the love of Jesus, what it is,
none but his loved ones know.

But *they know.*

There was an earthquake on the day Christ died on the cross. Not only do Matthew, Mark, and Luke all report that fact in their gospels, but fifteen hundred miles away in Rome, Tertullian wrote that on that day the sun was blacked out and the earth shook. In Greece Phlegon reported that "there was the greatest eclipse of the sun, and it became night in the sixth hour of the day (i.e., at noon), so that the stars even appeared in the heavens. There was a great earthquake and many things were overturned." That there was an earthquake on the day Christ died, there can be little doubt.

It is not suprising, then, that all three of the synoptic gospels should report such a cataclysmic event, as though the very earth trembled in horror at the atrocity being perpetrated on Calvary. What is surprising is that all three of the gospel writers should report only a single, seemingly minor bit of damage done by that earthquake. Probably many homes and public buildings and bridges and walls crumbled into piles of confused rubble, as the toll of such a major earthquake, but the three gospel writers report only this: that the curtain in the temple was torn in two, from the top to the bottom.

It was an impressive incident, demonstrating the force of nature, for that curtain was constructed of many thicknesses of woven cloth, and stretched from the floor to the high ceiling of the temple, and, in an instant, the force of the earthquake tore it completely in two, from top to bottom, as easily as one might rip a rotten dust cloth. And it demonstrated the capriciousness of nature. Not a stone, not a pillar, not a beam of that ninety-nine-year-old temple was disturbed: only that heavy, many-inches-thick curtain was torn in two.

But the real significance of the episode becomes clear when we remember that this was the curtain that hid from view the Holy of Holies, that most sacred spot in the temple where, presumably, God resided. And no one was permitted to go beyond that curtain into that most sacred presence except the high priest—and he only once a year on the Day of Atonement, to seek the forgiveness of the sins of the people.

But when Christ was crucified, that curtain was torn in two. He has become our high priest, who not only enters into God's most sacred presence, but also tears down the curtain so that we may go with him. Through Christ we have access to God!

The system of sacrificial offerings, as reported in the Old Testament, was a step above the practice in many pagan cultures that required the sacrifice of human beings to appease angry gods. As Paul wrote in his Roman letter, "I appeal to you therefore, brothers and sisters, by the mercies of God, to present your bodies as a living sacrifice" (Romans 12:1). It is a merciful God who requires not the sacrifice of a dead human being, but rather the service that can be rendered by the living.

But the Old Covenant required the offering of blood sacrifices, and the specifications of what kind of animal and the physical condition of the animal were carefully set forth. Generally speaking, the more valuable the animal and the better the physical condition of the animal, the more effective it was thought to be as a sacrificial offering to God.

But the system of sacrifices was inevitably a futile attempt to do what human beings can never accomplish. Even the most costly animal in the most robust condition was never quite enough to accomplish its intended purpose. Neither two heifers, nor two hundred, nor two thousand could buy forgiveness for human beings. Such offerings were simply the wrong currency.

The prophet Hosea realized this, and heard God saying, "I desire steadfast love and not sacrifice, the knowledge of God rather than burnt offerings" (Hosea 6:6). But the animal sacrifices continued, and people kept hoping that someday the perfect sacrifice would be found, one so pure and so utterly without flaw that its sacrifice would succeed in obtaining the favor of God.

It was in fulfillment of that hope that Jesus became our Paschal Lamb, our sacrifice, and it is through the utter surrender of that perfect life that Christ has given us, in his name, peace with God.

If you are a parent, you can surely remember when a child of yours asked for suggestions about a gift you might like to be given. And if you are like most parents, you probably said something like this: "I just want you to be a good and happy child, and to love me. That's all I want." And that's really all God wants from us.

DAY 126
Read Hebrews 11

After several chapters of rather tedious theological discussion, the writer now turns to the presentation of faith's hall of fame. Many of the towering figures of the Old Testament had won their place in this distinguished company because of their courageous obedience to the faith that possessed them. Despite the fact that not all the persons named were remembered as moral paragons (Jacob, for example, and the prostitute Rahab), all deserve to be included, because their faith in God led them to risk their homes, their families, even their very lives, to follow the lure of adventurous beliefs.

But toward the end of this pageant of Old Testament saints, the writer throws up his hands at the inevitable futility of trying to call every name on Faith's honor roll, but concludes by saying, "Time would fail me to tell of Gideon, Barak, Samson, Jephthah, of David and Samuel and the prophets—who through faith conquered kingdoms, administered justice, obtained promises, shut the mouths of lions, quenched raging fire, escaped the edge of the sword, won strength out of weakness, became mighty in war, put foreign armies to flight…" Surely if there were those who accomplished all these wonders in the name of faith, they deserved to be mentioned, at least.

But the fact is that there are unsung heroes of the faith in every generation, and few ever get their names in the daily paper, let alone on a page of scripture.

What qualifies people to be in Faith's Hall of Fame? It is surely a willingness to face incredibly difficult odds while holding on to the best you know. It is the stubborn belief that the darkest night will eventually yield to day. It is the conviction that patience in doing what is right will eventually win a victory, even when you are the only one who believes that. It is confidently accepting God-given tasks that would be impossible in human terms, and planning the victory celebration while everyone else is cutting up their underwear to make surrender flags. It is a willingness to stand absolutely alone, facing hostile hordes, for the sake of your loyalty to God. It is the unwavering belief that one person and God comprise a majority every time, everywhere.

There are still a few empty frames on Faith's Wall of Fame. Would your picture fit one of them?

Read Hebrews 12

The twelfth chapter of Hebrews begins with one of the most inspiring and challenging pictures of our Christian discipleship to be found anywhere. As Paul so often did, the writer of Hebrews employs an athletic metaphor to explain what the Christian life is all about. First there is the grandstand, filled with people who have previously won the race, and who now wear victors' crowns. And they are cheering and encouraging the runner on the racetrack below.

But the runner is severely handicapped because of weights that he must carry as he runs this race, and is likewise handicapped by memories of other races that he has run—and lost. And the lines on the track are blurred, and the right course is difficult to see and follow. And who is the runner at the focus of all this attention, preparing to run a difficult and demanding race? It is you.

Whoever you are, there is a great assemblage of witnesses who are watching you, praying for you, encouraging you, and believing in you. Every saint of the past is on your side and offering inspiration and comfort, for the victory they won is now in your hands, to win or lose. Carelessness or faithlessness could surrender what they bought with their courage and faith.

But you have handicaps even before you start this race. Doubts weigh heavily upon you. Temptations attempt to seduce you. The memory of other races that you ran—and lost—discourage you. You can't see the way clearly, and the distant goal is a blur. How can you achieve victory despite all these handicaps?

First, lay aside the weights and sins. Maybe you failed yesterday, but that was yesterday, and today is another day. Perhaps you are ashamed of past losses, but every day a new race is run. Now someone comes to help you remove those heavy weights and lay them aside. And since he went this way before you, he knows exactly how to lead you to victory. That one is Jesus Christ. He won the sweepstakes, and the reward was a seat in heaven beside God. And he's reserving the one beside him for you.

An elderly Scotswoman, who drew her meager living from selling grain in the open marketplace, was called upon by her pastor. She complimented him on his sermon at the kirk the previous Sunday. "And do you remember the title of the sermon, and the text?" the pastor quizzed her. She shook her head and replied, "I dinna ken the title nor the text, but I know this: I came right home and took the false bottom out of my bushel measure."

As she properly understood, faith experiences should result in some favorable changes in the way we live. What happens to us in our times of worship on Sunday in church should make some notable alterations in the way we conduct ourselves on Monday in the marketplace.

After a rather long and profound discussion of the concept of grace through faith in Christ, the writer of the Hebrew epistle now concludes the discussion by showing what evidence of that new life in Christ looks like. His ethical urgings do not suggest that the Christian life is defined by works that result in faith, but rather by faith that will inevitably result in good works.

The good works, which the writer lays as obligations upon his readers, begin with the admonition that we have an obligation, as Christians, to reach out to others in sympathy and helpfulness. We are to imitate Christ, who expressed unfailing compassion toward all people—believers and nonbelievers alike.

A seminary professor one day abandoned his lecture manuscript, leaned across his lectern and looked directly into the eyes of his students, and said, "Remember this, as you conduct your ministries: every person you meet on the road of life will be carrying some heavy burden. Many are doing it courageously, some sacrificially, but almost all of them will be carrying it secretly. And if you can't help them, for heaven's sake, don't hurt them."

Grace received becomes graciousness given. And although this human trait, alone, cannot result in our salvation, it is difficult to see how we can claim genuine salvation without bearing that fingerprint of Christ in our lives.

DAY 129
Read James 1

There is a term frequently used by astronomers that appears in this reading. It is the word *parallage,* which is translated "variation" in our New Testament but which, as the astronomers use the word, is translated "parallax." The dictionary defines parallax as "such difference in the apparent position of an object, specifically a star or other heavenly body, as would appear if it were viewed from two points." In other words, if an astronomer takes a picture of a star from one point, then takes another picture of the same star from another point, half a world away, the star's distance from the earth can be determined by geometric computation.

Or in photography: If you ever took a picture of a friend and when you got the picture back from the developer's, found that you had "cut the head off" your subject, you know that there is a slight difference between what you see through your viewer and what the camera takes a picture of through its lens. This difference is also called a parallax, and more expensive cameras compensate for that difference with a device known as a "parallax corrector."

So James says of God, "in whom there is no parallax" (1:17). In God there is no changeableness. Think of the implications of that realization! The God who strengthened Jesus to withstand his temptations is the same God who stands by you in your struggles, to help you resist. The God who heard Jesus' agonizing prayers in the Garden of Gethsemane hears your petitions when you experience your extremities. And the same God whom Jesus trusted to bring him safely through death and into a resurrection will be holding your hand and guarding your soul when the grim reaper calls for you.

And the same God who shows mercy to the saints also cherishes the souls of those who defy and ignore the heavenly presence. No matter what you are or what you have done, you cannot make God less than God is—and always was and always will be. God is not changed by our human circumstances. To put it simply: no matter where you are or what you are, you can always depend upon God to be God.

DAY 130
Read James 2

It has frequently been said that whereas Paul believed in salvation by faith, James claimed that salvation resulted from works. But that is a complete misunderstanding of both Paul and James. Yes, Paul did emphasize that salvation comes by grace, which we access through faith, but Paul also assured us that our faith would inevitably be revealed in our conduct. He said, "All of us must appear before the judgment seat of Christ, so that each may receive recompense for what has been done in the body, whether good or evil" (2 Corinthians 5:10). While our salvation is the free gift of God's grace, Paul argued, one cannot receive that gift without experiencing the gratitude that shows itself in living a godly life.

And certainly James did not claim that works alone would buy redemption for us. But James was writing his epistle to those who were already Christians. Obtaining salvation was no longer a matter of great concern for them. But James addressed himself to the subject that should have been their priority as Christians: How shall we live, now that we have received the redemption of Christ?

"We have faith," the people claimed. "All right," James responded, "how does it show in your life?" If there is no outward evidence of faith, one must wonder if it is really faith, or merely some false claim of it. How can faith be proved? "As the body without the spirit is dead, so faith without works is also dead" (v. 26). And a dead faith cannot save us.

Jesus himself said, "Not everyone who says to me, 'Lord, Lord,' will enter the kingdom of heaven, but only the one who does the will of my Father in heaven" (Matthew 7:21).

Both James and Paul would agree that faith and works are not opposites; they are the two sides of the same coin. And a coin with an authorized image engraved on only one side is counterfeit. So is any religious experience that does not include both faith and works.

DAY 131
Read James 3

One of the most frightening things Jesus ever said is recorded in the twelfth chapter of Matthew when he warned, "I tell you, on the day of judgment you will have to give an account for every careless word you utter; for by your words you will be justified, and by your words you will be condemned" (Matthew 12:36–37). If Jesus meant by those words that on the day of judgment we are going to have to sit and listen to a playback of every single thing we ever said, and give an accounting of it, in the terrible light of eternity, can you think of any further need of hell?

Especially in our day, when our arsenal of weapons has mostly dwindled to a collection of words, the spoken word has a frightening power to hurt. If we can recall those times in our own lives in which we were wounded the most grievously, weren't most of those occasions duels in which words were the weapons of choice?

But is it not also true that those experiences we most treasure consisted mostly of events in which certain words were spoken to us?—words like "I forgive you," or "I have good news for you," or, most blessed of all, "I love you." James was entirely right in declaring that the human tongue has greater power to wound or to bless than any other faculty we possess.

It is, therefore, more than a matter of proper elocution or courtesy that we must learn to discipline our tongues. It is a matter of living out the Christian faith. But most often, perhaps, it is when our tongues are silent that we sin the most grievously. "Set a seal upon my lips," the poet said. And that means that we should allow the Holy Spirit of God to prompt us to speak, when words are called for, or to be silent, when our silence would be the most compassionate gift we could offer.

If Jesus is listening to our every word—and our every silence—and if we are going to have to give an accounting of everything we said—or failed to say—on the day of judgment, isn't it urgent that we ask ourselves today, "What words can I speak today that will express the love of Christ to someone who needs to hear them?" And if there is a greater blessing in our remaining silent, when we are tempted to speak in anger or judgment, we must pray for the knowledge to know when silence is golden.

Read James 4

"Come now," James cautions us, "you who say, 'Today or tomorrow we will go to such and such a town and spend a year there, doing business and making money.' Yet you do not know what tomorrow will bring...Instead you ought to say, 'If the Lord wishes, we will live and do this or that.'" It is from that familiar passage that we have gleaned the phrase "the Lord willing." That phrase used to be heard more frequently than it is now, but it still crops up in conversation now and then, as Christian people look to the future and make their plans, but always in the realization that life is not a solitaire game, and other forces and purposes that we cannot know will play their part in the unfolding of our lives.

But however uncertain the future is, we do have today. Yesterday is gone. It is only a memory now, and however good or bad yesterday was, it is no longer ours. Tomorrow is only a dream, which may or may not be ours. But today is ours, and today offers quite enough challenges and resources to occupy us.

If we could see all the future, and could know all the difficulties and burdens that await us, we might be crushed and immobilized by the knowledge. But what we also can't see is the fact that with each fresh demand that faces us, there will be fresh resources with which to face it. Remember that it is useless to try to bear tomorrow's burdens today, for we will not get tomorrow's strength until tomorrow.

And remember this: if we could plan all our tomorrows, certain that all our plans would be fulfilled completely, we might thereby avoid some disappointments, but we would also deprive God of the delightful prerogative of surprising us with unexpected joys. Sometimes to make room in our lives for some blessing, God must interrupt our plans.

While our eyes tend to be focused upon the momentary, God is pledged to our ultimate good. And although we tend to prefer a smooth road, God prefers for us the road–rough or smooth–that leads to the right destination.

So when God's will differs from ours, and God's plans interrupt ours, we can take comfort in knowing that God stands taller, sees farther, and knows more than we do. And God loves us. Knowing that, we can be content to make all our plans with faith's qualification: "Deo volente"–the Lord willing.

Patience, as James asserts, is an essential attribute of the Christian. But sometimes what passes for patience is really only apathy or indifference. Remember that Jesus cared so deeply about the temple and felt so strongly about the injustice and corruption of the moneychangers in the temple that he drove them out with a whip. But that wasn't impatience. And it isn't patience when we are so lacking in social conscience that we can see injustices and dehumanizing acts of discrimination and disparagement without batting an eye or lifting a finger. That's not patience, it's apathy. And it's anything but Christian.

No, patience is really the consistent and faithful manner in which our faith, our hope, and our love continue to express themselves in our daily lives, regardless of the circumstances and difficulties we face in doing so.

There is a beautiful sentence, spoken by Jesus, that is more obscure than it deserves to be. It comes in the midst of a long series of instructions Jesus gave to his followers, about how they were to carry on his ministry. Jesus warned them that they would be persecuted, forsaken by friends, betrayed by families, threatened with martyrdom, and hated by many. Then Jesus offered them this beautiful advice: "In your patience possess ye your souls." (Luke 21:19, *King James Version*). The *New Revised Standard Version* translates it, "By your endurance you will gain your souls." There is some basis for believing that the *King James Version* is a more accurate translation: "In your patience possess ye your souls."

In other words, don't let your enemies steal away your soul by making you stoop to their level of behavior. If they hate you, they are blackening their own character. But if they succeed in making you hate them, you have relinquished control of your soul to them, and they have blackened it. If you have the courage and patience to remain Christian in every experience of your life, and clearly articulate that in your daily conduct, then you have retained control of your own soul. "Possess ye your souls."

In his magnificent hymn to love (1 Corinthians 13) Paul concludes by saying, "faith, hope, and love abide…" And that abiding power, that staying quality, that ferocious and stubborn refusal to let go of life's greatest treasures, is what patience is all about.

A group of boys were flying their kites in a park one day. The strong winds had carried the paper vessels far above the park until the low clouds swallowed them and made them seem to disappear. A man, watching the youthful play, began to tease one of the lads. "I see you have lost your kite," he said. "Oh, no," the boy replied, "it's still up there. You just can't see it." "But how do you know it's there if you can't see it?" the man asked. "Because," the boy replied, "I can feel the tug of it."

How can we believe in a God we cannot see? Because we can feel the tug of the divine in our lives.

As Peter wrote to these Christians he must have been keenly aware of the fact that he had an advantage that his readers did not. Peter had seen and known Christ in the flesh. It should have been easy for him to trust, with so many visible proofs of his faith. But even with that advantage, Peter still struggled to believe, and it took the miracle of the resurrection to make him a thoroughly convinced believer.

So Peter says, perhaps with admiration for them, or in regret for his own slowness to believe, "Although you have not seen him, you love him; and even though you do not see him now, you believe in him" (v. 8).

Perhaps Peter was remembering that Sunday evening, a week after Easter, when Jesus was tenderly dealing with the disappointing doubts of Thomas. Finally, after seeing the nail prints in Jesus' hands and side, Thomas fell to his knees and affirmed his faith. And Jesus said to him, "Have you believed because you have seen me? Blessed are those who have not seen and yet have come to believe" (John 20:29).

Jesus cherishes any sign of devotion on our part, however long it may have taken us to arrive at that point, and no matter what proofs it required. But Jesus has special praise for those who believe, in the absence of proof, and love a Lord they have not seen.

So Peter praises his first-century readers, as well as his twenty-first century readers. Faith that is substantiated by proof is no longer faith, but knowledge. Faith is the courageous willingness to stake our lives on that "tug" on our lives which is how the invisible God makes the divine presence known to us.

DAY 135
Read 1 Peter 2

Peter saw the Christian Church as the "New Israel." The Jews had failed to fulfill the responsibility for which God had chosen them: The Savior that the nation of Israel was to bring to the world was rejected by those to whom he was sent. So God found a "New Israel"—the church—which still bears that primary responsibility of bringing the Savior to the world.

In transferring that purpose to the Christians, God also transferred the honors that were to be earned by carrying the burden of being thus chosen. God had conferred two exalted titles upon the Jews. They were "a chosen race" and "a royal priesthood." They were not chosen to be given honor, but to bear a responsibility. And in fulfilling the responsibility they would be mediating between God and humanity. That is the role of a priest: to represent God to people, and to represent the people to God.

But now, the Christians have inherited both of these generous titles, plus one more. That short phrase is translated from a single Greek word, *laos*. That small word has a very rich and full meaning. Primarily it signifies "a people who have been given great honor and privilege because of the identity of their superior."

A man who has few possessions of great intrinsic value cherishes one small piece of furniture. It is a chair. It is not a comfortable chair to sit on, and the style in which it was crafted does not harmonize with any of the other furniture in his house. He has never been offered much money for it and would probably reject such offers if they were made. To him it is priceless, not because of what it is, but because of whose it was. It once belonged to former president Lyndon Johnson.

So our great value as persons is not, in any sense, a reflection of our own virtues or achievements, but results from our surrender to God, who gives us our worth.

Surprisingly, this word, *laos* is the root of our word "laity." Are you a laywoman or a layman? You have been given great honor, and the kingdom of God in this world and the church of Jesus Christ depend upon you! You are God's own people, and God is pleased to confer upon you significant authority and great honor. Though you may once have been "no people," now through the grace of our Lord Jesus Christ, you have ascended all the way to the top of human hopes and aspirations: "Now you are God's people!" (v. 10).

Remember who you are!

DAY 136
Read 1 Peter 3

Sally had come home from Sunday school in tears. After some patient questioning, the parents eventually learned that the cause of her tears was the memory verse the class had been taught that morning. It was 1 Peter 3:12, which reads, "The eyes of the Lord are upon the righteous." But what should have been a comforting thought seemed to her a threat: that God was always watching her, hoping to catch her misbehaving, to make a black mark against her. But her thoughtful parents gave her another translation, one that spoke the intended truth, but still gave her comfort: "The Lord loves you so much he can't keep his eyes off you!"

Here Peter is recalling Psalm 34, in which a portrait of a righteous person is presented, and to provide a stark contrast, an unrighteous person is defined. And while God's face is turned toward the righteous, "the face of the Lord is against those who do evil." Are we to understand from this teaching that God is partial to those who love and obey God? Does God "like" us when we are good, and "dislike" us when we are bad?

No, it means simply that those who defy God's laws are putting themselves in a position in which the whole universe will be their adversary. If a man thinks he can break the law of gravity, he is mistaken. He can only break himself by his disobedience, and thereby prove the validity of the law of gravity. But God still cares for the disobedient, just as the father in Jesus' parable continued to love the prodigal son, even after that arrogant young man had disappointed and grieved his father.

A mother of twelve was once asked which of her children she loved the most. The questioner expected her to say, "Oh, I love them all the same." Instead she replied, "I love most the one who's sick until he's well, and the one who's lost until he's back home."

God watches, in motherly concern, all the Earth's children. God watches over the righteous, eager to hear and answer their prayers, alert to any dangers through which God might guide and strengthen them, surrounding them with protective care. "God loves us so much he can't keep his eyes off us" when we are righteous.

In fact, God loves the righteous more than anyone, except for the unrighteous. The fact is, God loves each of us—the good as well as the bad—quite as though we were the only children God had.

DAY 137
Read 1 Peter 4

"Love covers a multitude of sins." This short but powerful sentence has entered the pantry of human expressions, so that although most people have used the expression, few realize its origin. It affirms the superiority of grace over law, of love over rules. Love does not measure out its gifts on fine scales. Love gives because that's its nature. Love hugs while law is still scrutinizing the rules to see if a handshake is warranted.

If we have genuine love for someone, we are willing to accept him, even though his frailties and faults may be obvious to us. That does not mean "love is blind." Love does not pretend that flaws are not present, but love is not defeated by those faults. Indeed, if we really love someone, love may require us to help her find extrication from the sins that may have ensnared her. But we do not demand recovery from such frailties before we can love the person.

In writing this word, could Peter have been thinking of Jesus' relationship with his twelve disciples? His magnanimous patience with them was a splendid illustration of the kind of love that "covers a multitude of sins." He endured the insipid and faithless stupidity of his disciples; he withstood the temper tantrums of James and John and the swaggering arrogance of Peter; he suffered the skepticism of Thomas and the betrayal of Judas. But, as the scripture points out, "having loved his own who were in the world, he loved them to the end" (John 13:1). And even though Peter's triple denial of Jesus must have hurt, Jesus was waiting–on the other side of the resurrection–to restore Peter's faith and confidence by giving him a triple opportunity to reaffirm his love for his master.

An elementary school teacher was laboring to introduce to her students the concept of fractions. Finally she utilized an illustration that she thought might make it all clear. "If there were seven members of your family," she asked, "and if you had one pie for dinner, how many pieces would your mother cut the pie into?" "Six," one child answered promptly. "No," the teacher said, "I'm afraid you don't know your fractions." "But you don't know my mother," the child replied. "Because if there were seven members of my family, and we had only one pie, my mother would say she didn't want any."

That's love–illogical, incomprehensible love–and it covers a multitude of sins.

It is not unusual to hear small children in Sunday school misquote a familiar sentence in this chapter, which says, in the *King James Version,* "He careth for thee" (v. 7). Perhaps because they have heard their parents' repeated admonitions about eating their vegetables, the tots sometimes inadvertently render that memory verse, "Eat carrots for me!"

But as useful as that "Revised Substandard Version" might be to parents in intimating to their children that even the Bible demands that they eat their vegetables, it is clear that an even more valid truth is contained in these few words: "He cares about you."

Several years ago a submarine, submerged in deep waters, was damaged severely when a torpedo was accidentally detonated. The resulting damages made it impossible for the submarine to surface, and the radio's communication center was affected. Water was entering the hull through a breach caused by the explosion. Help was urgently needed, and the communications officer continued to send out pleas for help, not knowing whether the transmitter was getting the messages through. "Does anybody know we're here?" the messages continued to be sent. "Does anybody care?"

Though those aboard the submarine had no way of knowing it, the pleas had been heard. Help was on the way, and rescue was imminent. Someone cared about them!

Those long and excruciating minutes that passed before the rescue was effected provide a painful picture of the existential anxieties that are the inevitable consequence of life in a world that knows trouble and sorrow, but often does not realize that there is a Deliverer who knows what we are going through, and cares.

When we know that God cares about us, we are thereby released from the fretful anxieties that make life a painful ordeal for many people. There is a certain security that results from our belief that the great God of the universe is watching us with tender care, ready to provide whatever we need to achieve victory in our struggles.

DAY 139
Read 2 Peter 1

In Jesus' parable of the talents (Matthew 25:14–30) our Lord made a surprising and puzzling statement: "To all those who have, more will be given...; but from those who have nothing, even what they have will be taken away." At first glance that seems a cynical view of the way things work in this world. "Them that has, gets," we say; "the rich get richer and the poor get poorer." But a moment's thought reveals the truth of Jesus' assessment. He who has only a little patience will invariably lose what patience he has. But one who has great patience will find his store of that virtue growing as he uses it. One who loves little will eventually find his short supply of it altogether exhausted, but one who loves much will discover his resource of love multiplied.

Peter, in expanding on this concept, shows how faith must be invested, or it will be lost. We must add to our faith, or our faith will be subtracted from us.

But how are we to add to (or invest) our faith? Peter suggests a pattern of growth. First, we must add to our faith knowledge. Most of us come to Christ not as a consequence of study, but as an emotional response of the will to the inviting Christ. At that point, we may know very little about the Christian faith, and that is understandable. But we must not remain at that point. The first step in cultivating our faith is knowledge. We must do our best, Paul urged us (2 Timothy 2:15), to prove ourselves to God by our study of the holy word. It is understandable if a four-year-old cannot read the Bible. But if a forty-year-old doesn't read the Bible, his growth as a Christian is stunted.

Self-control is the next step in the growth of our faith. Although the Holy Spirit in our lives is inclined to lead us into all virtue, we still hold all moral decisions in our hands. Discipline is the necessary investment of our faith in the focused effort that will keep our faith strong and effective in our own life.

The next step in the maturation of our faith is steadfastness. That means being faithful to the highest we know, even when doubts assail or discouragement frustrates us. Godliness is the next step in the growth of our faith. As we come to know God, we also come to resemble God in our attitudes. Then brotherly/sisterly affection will surely follow, as we share with God the respect and concern for all human life.

Faith is a living thing, and like all living things, it grows or it dies.

There is a stark and terrible warning in these words of Peter: "It would have been better for them never to have known the way of righteousness than, after knowing it, to turn back from the holy commandment that was passed on to them" (v. 21). This stern admonition was directed against those who had once begun a life of Christian discipleship, then abandoned that effort. Such defections have always saddened and weakened the whole church, for such people seem to be "dissatisfied customers" of the Christian experience.

But why should it be worse for those people than for those who have never known the right way? Because if one has never heard the Christian gospel, he cannot be blamed for not responding to it. But if one has heard the call of Christ and, after a preliminary step toward faith, then deliberately turns and goes in the opposite direction, his action is an unforgivable insult to the Son of God.

Jesus was especially clear in his condemnation of such defections. He said, "No one who puts a hand to the plow and looks back is fit for the kingdom of God" (Luke 9:62). And Jesus seemed especially grieved about the rich man who, having approached Jesus, then turned away because the cost of discipleship seemed too great to him (Mark 10:17–22).

But most of us do not face the temptation of actual heresy or deliberate defection, but rather the danger of drifting away from an earlier commitment.

Preachers are sometimes guilty of painting temptation in lurid, dramatic colors, as though in one desperate act of deliberate wickedness, we fall to the depths of degradation. But the fact is that for the most part temptation whispers instead of shouting. Sin's seductive invitation urges not a descent all the way to hell, but only an inch or so below our current position.

Like the gradual depreciation of a house, so the decay of our souls is equally slow and, most of the time, barely perceptible. No one ever sets out to become an alcoholic. It just happens—one little sip at a time. And no one ever chooses, deliberately, to be bitter or dishonest or immoral. Each of those unhappy destinies is achieved through small steps that seemed, at the time, to be going in no particular direction.

It is a beneficial, possibly redemptive, but frequently sobering exercise to look up occasionally from the path you are following, to ask, "Where is this road leading? And if I follow this path to its end, will I wind up where I really wanted to be, when sunset comes?"

DAY 141
Read 2 Peter 3

Many people who lived at the time of the writing of this epistle still had not learned the lesson of Jonah. But for that matter, neither have many people in this day.

Jonah, who is usually identified as a Minor Prophet, might better be thought of as a "Minus Prophet," for most of the lessons to be derived from his story are learned from Jonah's mistakes. All the conclusions to be drawn from his story are valuable, but none more than the final one: We have no basis for complaint when God exhibits more mercy and patience than we think is justified.

Jonah, after trying unsuccessfully to run away from God, finally came to Nineveh to inform the people of that sinful city that God would punish their wickedness by destroying their city. To Jonah's complete surprise (and disappointment) the whole city repented and turned to God. Now, God had promised Jonah a spectacular demonstration of divine wrath, and Jonah found a ringside seat from which to enjoy the fireworks. But no fireworks came, and Jonah was angry. How dare God disappoint him by withholding the fireworks? But God answered Jonah's petulant complaint by saying, "Should I not pity Nineveh...?" It is always a mistake to underestimate God's mercy.

What does the story of Jonah have to do with the Second Epistle of Peter? Simply this: many people of the time of this epistle had made the same mistake of which Jonah was guilty. There were many who thought Christ's second coming had been too long delayed. As a result, there were three prevailing opinions. First, there were those who assumed that the long delay of the coming of Christ made that expected event even more imminent. Second, some saw God's apparent tardiness in fulfilling the divine prophecy as proof that such a cataclysmic event would never occur, and that this long-held belief could be safely discarded.

Finally, there were those who saw the days and centuries that had come and gone with no evidence of the coming of the Lord as proof that God had failed to do what had been promised and could, therefore, no longer be trusted.

And now, many centuries later, there are still people who incline toward one or more of those opinions. But all three opinions reveal the same mistake God sought to correct in Jonah. And the same word God spoke to Jonah needs to be heard again. We must never make the mistake of trying to make God conform to our schedule, or to our formula for access to heaven. However patient and however merciful you may think God to be, you must understand that God is a million times more patient and merciful than Jonah–or we–could imagine.

DAY 142
Read 1 John 1

The passage of two millennia has obscured some details about this lovely little epistle known as First John. But of some presumptions we may be reasonably sure. It is likely that this document was written by an elderly Christian minister, who was quite possibly the last human being alive who could claim a personal relationship with Jesus in our Lord's span of years in this world. He had seen Jesus with his own eyes, felt his hand, heard his spoken word.

And now, near the end of a most productive ministry, he felt the need to warn his many friends and followers of certain problems that were threatening the life of the church. Among the dark clouds on the church's horizon was a noticeable decline of fervor among the Christians. Generations had passed with no sign of Christ's return. The Roman Empire still held the world in its grip, and demonstrated its paranoid fear of dissent by persecuting the Christians. Philosophical and theological fads attracted the attention of many who seemed convinced that what was new was necessarily better.

Perhaps the most frightening problem of all was the tendency, on the part of some Christians, to try to find some accommodation, some superficial hybrid, combining the tenets of the Christian faith and the popular beliefs and assumptions of the secular world.

The distinction between what was Christian and what was worldly had gotten fuzzy, somehow, and it was no longer easy to know the difference.

But John proposed a test to determine what was true and what was false in the religious lives of the readers of his letter. Let every person ask herself or himself: No matter how much I may claim the name of Christ, do my actions prove my fellowship with Christ, or deny it? One can no more have fellowship with Christ and continue to commit the sins that betray him than a man can really love his wife if he maintains liaisons with a succession of other women.

But John hastens to reassure us that while we may seek sinlessness as an ideal, we are unlikely ever to achieve that blessed state of complete innocence in this world. "If we say that we have no sin, we deceive ourselves, and the truth is not in us" (v. 8). But John wants us to know that even if we are vulnerable to the tempter's snares, we need not continue forever to bear the responsibility for our sins. "If we confess our sins, he who is faithful and just will forgive us our sins and cleanse us from all unrighteousness" (v. 9).

So spoke an old pastor who had discovered these truths in his own life.

One cannot help but be struck by the affectionate spirit of this lovely letter. "My little children," John addresses his readers. Here is a diminutive reference which does not belittle, but rather caresses the reader with the tender affection of the writer. What can account for this sentimentality?

Perhaps it was due to John's age. While we have no documentation of this, it has been suggested by biblical scholars across the centuries that John was the last surviving apostle. Indeed, he was probably the only one of the twelve whose life was not forfeited in martyrdom. It is not unreasonable to assume that John's readers were people whom the old pastor had known throughout their lives. He had seen them grow up. He had observed their mistakes and, perhaps, had prayed for their forgiveness. He cheered their achievements; he regretted—but understood—their mistakes. Above all, he continued to love them, and to pray for them. What a contribution he must have made to the lives of those "little children" of his, who were the recipients of his fatherly care!

Unfortunately, such gentle wisdom does not accrue as a dividend to the process of aging. Not all elderly people are kind and understanding. As a matter of unfortunate fact, some people become bitter and judgmental as they grow old. Sometimes we are tempted to forget our own youthful peccadilloes in our wholesale condemnation of the younger generation. One's age is no guarantee of virtue.

But what a beautiful masterpiece of character is an older person who still thinks optimistically, still encourages and affirms others, still sees something to praise in the young, and still prays for them.

In the bleak days of the Battle of Dunkirk a young British soldier was wounded and brought to a first aid tent. The attending doctor sought to engage the soldier in conversation, to determine the clarity of his thinking. "Are you all right?" the doctor inquired. "Yes, and I will get well again," the youth said, "because my grandmother is praying for me."

And many a youth has found shelter from trouble and courage against temptation by remembering that some old man or woman—a grandparent, perhaps—was praying for them. And that's a ministry anyone can perform.

"See what love the Father has given us, that we should be called children of God" (v. 1). Thus John identifies one of the most striking and encouraging attributes of our God. We have a Lord who wants to share with us the divine name and all the prerogatives suggested by it.

A short story, which used to be found in elementary school reading books, bore the name of "The Great Stone Face." In that story, a boy named Ernest grew up within a short distance of a rocky bluff that appeared to have a face etched on it. It was a strong face, a rugged face, but a face that seemed to reflect the attitude of the one who looked upon it. All through his childhood and youth Ernest daily studied that face until, as the story related, Ernest came to have the same facial features and expression as the great stone face. He had become what he admired.

So when we companion with God, we find ourselves taking on the attributes of God. And God welcomes that transformation, and, indeed, makes it possible by providing for us the power by which we accomplish that.

In the days in which this letter was written, it was common for parents to take a newborn child to the priest in the temple to give the child a name. And in so doing, they expressed their hopes for that child, and also declared their claim as the parents of the child.

So God has given us a name—we are the children of God. And in giving us that name, God has expressed the highest hopes for our lives: that we should bear the marks of our relationship. But in giving us the name, God has also demonstrated his claim on our lives.

But John says that we not only have the name (given magnanimously by God, before we deserve such a distinction), but we also have the reality. "And that is what we are!" John says. We may not look like it at times. We may not act like it. We may not talk like it. But unless we renounce our relationship with God by deliberate intent, God will continue to love us and provide for us and plan for us as children of the divine. Claim your inheritance!

DAY 145

In this chapter John reaches the highest point of his letter, and tells us, in effect, the best thing we can know about God, and the best thing we can know about ourselves. "God is love," the text says (v. 8), thus giving us the shortest—and perhaps the truest—definition of our God. That simple three-word sentence tells us all we need to know about our freedom of will. It was because God is love that the Creator gave us the right to determine our own destiny. Had God not loved us that much, we might have been made puppets of some superior intelligence. But God loved us enough to trust us with freedom.

And because God is love, God has promised to provide for us. God did not give us life and then leave us to fend for ourselves. God is constantly watching over us, to assure that we have all the resources we need for life to be abundant. Jesus said, "Do not worry, saying 'what will we eat?' or 'what will we drink?' or 'what will we wear?'… your heavenly father knows that you need all these things" (Matthew 6:31). And knowing that we need them is all the motivation God needs to provide them, because God is love, and love cannot watch impassively while the one loved remains in need.

And because God is love, Christ died for us, to secure forgiveness of our sins and eternal life. "God proves his love for us in that while we still were sinners Christ died for us" (Romans 5:8). Christ on the cross was divine love in action.

Heaven itself is evidence of the fact that God is love. How could a loving God allow the injustices and tragedies of this life to have the last word? Because God is the very essence of love, we can expect the Creator to provide a last chapter of life that will give eternal proof that God cares about us.

But this teaching also tells us the best thing we can know about ourselves. Whatever our faults or frailties or mistakes, we are people whom God loves, and that distinction is the one fact that gives us the greatest hope. No material wealth, no physical health, no social or political status, no mental acuity can come within a million miles of this best thing you can know about yourself: You are a person who is deeply loved by the God of the Universe!

DAY 146

A theology professor stood before his class on the first day of a new semester. He studied the students over the tops of his spectacles before giving his traditional warning: "Beloved, we are about to engage in the study of theology, and, believe me, it will be no picnic. Strong men have wept bitter tears over this stuff, and a few have gone quite permanently mad. If anyone here has enrolled in this study under the erroneous assumption that it is a snap course, he has let himself in for something that he would gladly exchange for leprosy within a week." A bit extreme, perhaps, but an appropriate introduction to a difficult subject. And what a slander it would have been against a distinguished study to pretend that theology is simple and undemanding. It was not only honest but also appropriate to disabuse the students of the notion that such a course would require little of those who undertook it.

One is shocked, then, to read John's word that "God's commandments are not burdensome" (v. 3). Tell that to Paul, who endured beatings, stonings, whippings, imprisonment, and slanders. Tell that to John, who was torn from his home and confined to the penal isle of Patmos. Tell that to the martyrs of every age, who have not shrunk from persecution because of their faith. Tell that to the Christians in the People's Republic of China, who continue to live valiant and courageous Christian lives, in defiance of the repression imposed upon them by their government. Many things may be said in truth about the Christian life, but whoever says it is an easy path has deluded himself. If you think the commandments of God are not burdensome, then perhaps you have not yet picked it up.

Why, then, does John insist that "the commandments of God are not burdensome"?

It is because those who willingly carry the burden of discipleship do so out of love for God. And love makes any burden bearable, any pain tolerable. It's like the poster boy for Boys' Town, willingly carrying a crippled lad on his shoulders. "He ain't heavy, mister, he's my brother!" Love makes the difference. And if we love God, the divine commandments are not heavy, either.

DAY 147
Read 2 John

"The Elder and the Elect Lady" sounds as if it might have been the title of a movie starring Humphrey Bogart and Katharine Hepburn. One suspects, however, that those two designations might reveal an even more exciting reality. Who were "The Elder" and "The Elect Lady"?

The title "Elder" generally referred to a supervising officer of a local congregation. It is clear, however, from the content of the letter that this elder was writing from a distance, and that he felt that he had the authority to speak on behalf of a larger constituency of congregations. We know that the term "elder" had come to be both an ecclesiastical designation and an affectionate title. Peter referred to himself as "a fellow elder" in his first epistle (1 Peter 5:1). Peter would certainly command a more prestigious title, if we were to take this reference as a title of ecclesiastical authority. So we might assume that whoever wrote this letter modestly identified himself by a term that implied not great authority, but an affectionate relationship with his readers.

"The elect lady" could refer to a woman of importance. The word in Greek, *eklekte,* has become a name in common usage, "Electra." But from the body of this short letter we learn that the writer is addressing a whole congregation. So "the bride of Christ" is given yet another feminine designation: "the elect lady," a fellowship of those who had been called (or elected) to Christian sainthood.

It is a beautiful thing to think of oneself as "elect." It is not so much our choice as Christ's, that we have become his followers. Our decision only confirms his. Our commitment "seconds the motion" made by Christ.

So an aged Christian saint, much loved by his many followers, writes this lovely little letter to a congregation composed of people whom Christ has called to discipleship. And what does he tell them? Beware of false teachers, and be careful that you do not, in reckless negligence, let your eternal treasure slip out of your hand.

DAY 148
Read 3 John

There is sufficient evidence to suggest that both this short letter and its immediate predecessor came from the same writer, but whereas the second epistle was addressed to a whole congregation (referred to as "the elect lady") the third is written to an individual named Gaius. There are three other men with that same name in the New Testament records, but it is extremely unlikely that this Gaius could be identified with any of the other three. Gaius was, in fact, the most common name in the Roman Empire in those days.

But the writer, while warmly commending Gaius for his radiant spiritual health, lays upon him a special responsibility. Christian missionaries were on their way, and the Elder intercedes on their behalf, requesting that Gaius and his congregation provide hospitality for the missionaries. Further, the writer hopes that Gaius and his fellow Christians "send them on their journey as befits God's service"–that is, with a generous offering in their pockets to finance their missionary endeavors. Though different euphemisms are employed in different ages, the "missionary offering" has remained an essential part of the life of a congregation. And why not? For starting with Paul, Christian missionaries have, as a rule, with cheerful and courageous hearts accepted hardship, persecution, and danger as inevitable elements in their ministries. It is only fair that those of us who cling to the comforts of home be willing, at least, to share in the cost of the Christian enterprise to which they have given their lives.

Nor is it unheard of that there would be those in the congregation–as there were in the congregation of Gaius–who oppose such offerings and the mission supported by them. Not only do they refuse to give such support, they resent the support given by others, and attempt to freeze such people out of the church. These dog-in-the-manger church folk did not die out in the early history of the church. They are still to be found in every congregation that seeks to provide some conscientious response to Christ's great commission. But all such individuals receive John's bitterest judgment (v. 11): "Whoever does evil has not seen God."

DAY 149

Face it: this is a world in which ships do sink, airplanes crash, and mountain climbers fall. Bad things do happen, even to some very good people—even devout Christian people. We simply cannot avoid danger. It is inherent in life. And the function of the Christian faith is not to blind us to the dangers, nor to give us some kind of naïve expectation that if we trust God, God will not allow anything bad to happen to us. No one ever had a stronger faith than Jesus, and look what happened to him!

But our faith makes it possible for us to live valiantly, confidently, hopefully, and victoriously, despite the dangers and risks.

Many of us have an inborn fear of falling. Even newborn infants experience that fear. And psychologists tell us that this dread takes on a new dimension when we grow up and achieve a certain stature in life. In our secret lives we feel a gnawing dread that we might fall from the position we occupy, or the reputation we have earned. There is a "fear of falling" that haunts all of us.

How wonderfully refreshing it is, then, to turn to one of the Bible's least-read books, Jude, and to read there this wonderful sentence, "Now to him who is able to keep you from falling, and to make you stand without blemish in the presence of his glory with rejoicing, to the only God our Savior, through Jesus Christ our Lord, be glory, majesty, power, and authority, before all time and now and forever, Amen" (v. 24).

Those words, as moving as they are in English, are insipid beside the Greek words that Jude originally used. *"To de dynameno!"* it says. That word *dynameno* is the word from which Alfred Nobel derived the word "dynamite." It says, literally, that this God whom we trust is dynamite, and is able and willing to use all that dynamic power of his to keep us from falling flat on our faces. There is something solid and dependable that surrounds us in life, something of substance on which we can bounce. Yes, there are still infinite ways in which we can stumble, and we will continue to do so, for the Divine has not used his dynamic power to take away our freedom. But the solid, strong power of God works in our favor, heals our bruises, and sets us ultimately back on our feet.

There are two words whose meaning we must understand before we can make much sense of the mysterious book of Revelation. The first is the word apocalyptic. In the broadest sense, apocalyptic includes all religious literature that abounds in visions of God or revelations from God concerning the end of the present, evil age. Included in this genre of literature are sections of Joel, Zechariah, Daniel, Ezekiel, and certain teachings of Jesus (Matthew 24 and 25) and the fourth chapter of 1 Thessalonians. Such literature is always concerned with the end of the present age, with a final, decisive battle between the forces of good (often referred to as "the children of light") and the forces of evil ("the children of darkness.") The closest parallel in modern literature is the science-fiction story. But it should be noted that apocalyptic literature is not fiction. It is, rather, the truth presented in a different way—with symbols and omens and mystical events to suggest (rather than speak) the truth.

The second word that must be understood is cryptographic. The book of Revelation is written partially in code, by using symbols and events with which the intended readers would be familiar, but which would be meaningless to those who were not acquainted with those symbols.

So the apocalyptic, cryptographic book of The Revelation to John uses the format of a letter to seven congregations, then incorporates a mystical view of heaven, the future of the earth, and God's eternal reign as a means of reassuring Christians who were facing the determined persecution of the Roman Empire.

Summed up in a single phrase: the book of Revelation seeks to prove that this is, after all, God's world, and regardless of how things look from day to day, God is in charge, and that which is right and good will ultimately prevail.

Theologian Reinhold Niebuhr used to say, "I'll be a pessimist with you, year by year, if you'll be an optimist with me, age by age." So says the cryptic book of Revelation.

In the second and third chapters of Revelation, a message is sent by the Risen Christ to each of the seven churches in Asia Minor to which the writing was addressed. And in each case Christ says—presumably to John, who was acting as the heavenly stenographer—"To the angel of the church in Ephesus," or "To the angel of the church in Smyrna," or Pergamum, or Laodicea or Philadelphia, or one of the others, "write this." The intended picture is that there is a divine presence in each church, something utterly and completely beyond the combined attributes and efforts of the human beings who constitute its membership.

The idea of a "guardian angel," despite the sentimental fluff that surrounds the concept in our day, is based on biblical teaching. Daniel taught that the angel (or prince) Michael was the guardian of Israel. Daniel credited his own deliverance from the lions' den to the presence of an angel with him. He wrote, "My God sent his angel and shut the lions' mouths" (Daniel 6:22). Even Jesus expressed the belief that children are watched over by their angels. He said, "Take care that you do not despise one of these little ones; for, I tell you, in heaven their angels continually see the face of my Father in heaven" (Matthew 18:10).

So whether the image of the guardian angel of persons or churches should be taken literally or figuratively, the inescapable truth is that God has arranged for a divine presence to watch over everyone, and every church. That divine presence may be thought of as the spiritual conscience of the church, or the honor of the church. That divine presence has been invited by the thousands of times the Holy Spirit has been invoked. And now that God has answered those prayers, and has stationed an angel at the altar of the church, what must we do about it? Can you ever again neglect or belittle the church, when you know that divine presence is there?

And what difference will it make to your life to know that there is a guardian angel assigned by heaven to protect you and to guide you into all righteousness? And what will that angel do if you grieve the Spirit by rebelling against God's will for your life?

Did you ever imagine an angel weeping?

Following the message to each of the seven churches there is the exhortation, "Let anyone who has an ear listen to what the Spirit is saying to the churches" (v. 6). Note that it does not say, "listen to what the Spirit says to this church" or to "that church." The implication is that all the approbation and criticism directed to all seven of the churches are applicable to all people. Within every one of us there is something of the patient endurance of the Ephesians, but we also share with that church the flagging of spirit that denotes a cooling of the love for Christ that we once had.

Like the Christians at Smyrna we also face the possibility of tribulation and trouble, and need to arm ourselves with costly faithfulness against the uncertainties of the future.

Like the members of the Pergamum congregation we have demonstrated a certain depth of loyalty, but while stoutly defending our faith against external difficulty, we have been oblivious to the encroachment of false teachings within ourselves. And similar to the Christians at Thyatira, our record of discipleship is a mixed bag of faithfulness and carelessness, stoutly holding the line against evil in some matters, but opening our embrace wide to accept other evils.

And we bear a family likeness to the church at Sardis, whose religious experience had to be expressed in the past tense. And the Philadelphia Christians are our brothers and sisters under the skin, for we, too, feel powerless in the face of the monstrous evils in our day, but we frequently allow our self-pity over small resources to keep us from doing what we can do, and ought to do, to establish the reign of God where we are.

And who of us (and which of our churches) does not suffer the Laodicea syndrome, being neither completely committed nor utterly disaffected, but just halfway between. Lord help us if our lack of commitment disgusts God as much as Laodicea's did!

But with all the seven churches we see a sign of great hope and God's extravagant patience: there is before us an open door, which God has opened, and no one can shut. Whether we go through that door into God's presence is a decision each of us makes.

Now there is a dramatic shift in the scenery, from the rigors and uncertainties of Earth, to the indescribable glories of heaven. The Seer of Patmos is given a glimpse of the eternal residence of the God of all the universe and those whom God has chosen to share those precincts for all time. And the first feature John notes in that unfolding panorama is a door. A door serves two functions: it keeps out those who are not wanted and opens wide to admit those who are welcome.

Jesus identified himself as a door: "I am the door," he said (John 10:7, 9, KJV). Earlier in Revelation the risen Christ is heard saying, "Listen, I am standing at the door, knocking; if you hear my voice and open the door, I will come in to you and eat with you, and you with me" (Revelation 3:20). Jesus is our access, our ticket of admission, our key that opens the lock of the door to heaven.

Pure fiction, to be sure, but suggestive of a glorious truth is the tale about St. Peter, the guardian of the pearly gates, who began to notice people in the heavenly company whom he could not remember having admitted. Their robes were soiled and their haloes were askew. It gradually dawned on the saintly gatekeeper that heaven's security had been breached, and that undocumented aliens were somehow gaining admittance.

One night, therefore, after the gates had been closed and locked for the night, Peter hid behind a pillar to watch. Finally, to his astonishment, he saw a shadowy figure approach the gate and—though the weight of the gate ordinarily required the strength of several angels to open it—the lone figure was able, with the expenditure of great energy, to open the gate just the width of one person. Then a long parade of souls entered heaven, each one welcomed with a warm embrace from the opener of the gate.

Indignantly St. Peter emerged from his hiding place to confront the unauthorized opener of the gate. It was Jesus! "Please let them in, Peter," the Christ pled. "They are so tired. I know their robes are a bit dirty, and their haloes are a little crooked. But they are special friends of mine, and I love them."

Fanciful, perhaps, but the story has a ring of truth. Who of us is so sure of our self-won righteousness that we would not be in need of the special mercy of the loving, accepting Christ who offers himself as our personal door to heaven?

DAY 154

Read Revelation 5

It is clear that the writer of Revelation was familiar with the apocalyptic writings of the Old Testament, such as the prophetic book of Ezekiel. In the second chapter of that book, the prophet wrote, "I looked, and a hand was stretched out to me, and a written scroll was in it. He spread it before me; it had writing on the front and on the back, and written on it were words of lamentation and mourning and woe" (Ezekiel 2:9). It is obvious that John's vision was, in part, shaped by his memory of this symbolic story.

But there is one aspect of John's vision that does not have roots in Ezekiel: the seven seals. According to Roman law, a person's will was written on a scroll; then the scroll was signed by seven witnesses, after which the scroll was rolled up, and each of the seven witnesses tied a thread around the rolled-up scroll, and the thread was sealed at the knots with sealing wax.

So John's vision of heaven begins with a picture amalgamated from a Hebrew prophecy and a Roman law. But from that palette of contrasting colors the Seer paints a profoundly meaningful picture of the future. It tells us, first of all, that the writing covered both sides of the scroll, which suggests that the future is complicated and crowded. There is both good and bad in the future, together with all the shadings in between. To those who will be looking for good things, there will be good things to be found, but those people who insist upon seeing evil will find sufficient evil to satisfy their lusts. Blessings and cataclysms will be in the future, as well—fragrant flowers and noxious weeds will grow side by side in that garden.

The scroll of the future is sealed; no one can be found who can break all those seals to find what the future has in store.

But the message of great encouragement to be found in this picture is not what is in the scroll, but rather what the scroll is *in*. It is held firmly in the right hand of God. As the song puts it, "We may not know what the future holds, but we know who holds the future."

"The Four Horsemen of the Apocalypse" was a title given to four especially competent football players at Notre Dame. The reference, of course, was to this chapter of Revelation, in which the Lamb (representing Jesus Christ) is found worthy to open the seven seals on the scroll of the future. And when each of the first four seals was opened, there came forth a horse and rider, each one distinct in color and meaning.

The first was a white horse, whose rider wore a crown. He carried a bow, and he went forth to conquer. The coffers of the Roman Empire were kept filled by means of the conquests of its armies. No more honorable purposes were claimed for these conquests. Condensed to its simplest form, war is murder and theft. Even in those instances in which war is apparently made inevitable by the irresponsible and bloodthirsty acts of injustice by some demigod, war is still always a tragedy. And as this first seal on the scroll of the future indicates, war will continue to plague us in the generations to come.

When the second seal was opened, there emerged a blood-red horse, whose rider carried a great sword, and whose goal was to deprive the earth of peace. The human family was not very old when one of its first sons rose up in anger and killed his brother. And the internecine rivalry and strife have continued. When we realize that God regards all people everywhere as a family, we must accept the fact that every breath of hatred and every struggle is a fight between brothers. And as that tragedy has haunted our past, so will it prey upon our future.

The third seal's removal released a black horse, whose grim rider carried a set of scales, and whose report of unreasonably high prices indicated a famine.

And resulting from the conquest, the hatred, and the famine, the fourth rider—a pale horse and rider—came forth to stalk the world in the robes of death: the grim reaper.

Such were the evil conditions present in the chaotic world in which the Seer and his Christian readers lived. "In the world," Jesus said, "ye shall have tribulation" (John 16:33, KJV). The Four Horsemen tell us nothing that we haven't already observed in our world. But remember that this is, after all, God's world, and that beyond all the tears and fears, God will be there, waiting for us with comfort and peace.

DAY 156
Read Revelation 7

With an exquisite sense of timing and suspense, the writer of Revelation leads us through the opening of the sixth seal, and with breathless alertness we await the denouncement that surely will be revealed when the seventh seal is removed. But it is precisely when our curiosity is at its peak that John takes a recess. But that brief recess tells us something about the magnificent patience of God.

Just as we reach the point in this symbolic narrative when the Earth is about to be destroyed, we are given a glimpse of the last-minute effort of God to ensure that all the children of God are marked for eternal life. "Hold the curtains," God says compassionately to the angels whose destructive forces are about to be unleashed on the earth. "I want to make sure all my children are present and accounted for."

So begins the final calling of the roll. First the ranks of the children of Israel are polled. From every tribe of Israel they come, one hundred forty-four thousand of them.

And notice that God reports this canvass of Jewish believers in a Jewish way of numbering: one-hundred forty-four would be quickly recognized by Hebrew people as the product of twelve times twelve times one thousand. Twelve (twice the human number of six) meant everybody—the whole world. Then multiply that number by itself, then again raise it by a factor of a thousand and what you wind up with is an unimaginably great number. Those who insist upon taking this number literally, and claim that only one hundred forty-four thousand people will get to heaven, have missed a magnificent point. What God is saying here is that there is room in heaven for everybody. And his brother. And his sister.

Then God considers the other children of heaven, those who cannot claim a Jewish ancestry. And the number of those was equally staggering: "a great multitude that no one could count" (v. 9).

God has more children than any of us suspect, and in the eternal joy God has planned for that great family, there is always room for one more.

Such is the convoluted formulation of the book of Revelation that when at last the seventh seal is opened, what is revealed is another series of seven. This time it is seven angels, each one with a trumpet. These angels were well known to the people of Israel, for their names (Uriel, Raphael, Raguel, Michael, Sariel, Gabriel, and Remiel) were reported in the Apocryphal book of Tobit. They were archangels, and enjoyed the privilege of standing in the very presence of God. And they were given trumpets, which meant that they were "announcing angels." Remember that it was the angel Gabriel who "announced" to Mary that she was to bear a son of the Holy Spirit. This same Gabriel is frequently envisioned as the angel whose trumpet blast will announce the coming of the Lord at the last day. And Paul spoke of the day when the trumpet will sound, and the dead will be raised (1 Corinthians 15:52).

Although there is no detailed correlation, the dire natural catastrophes announced by the angels are reminiscent of the plagues that were visited upon Pharaoh, to "persuade" Pharaoh to release the people of Israel from their bondage. It is possible that the Seer of Patmos wanted his readers to see the similarities here. The predicted hail, fire, water-turning-to-blood, darkness covering the land, and other plagues might have been seen as God's last-ditch effort to warn people, and to convince them to turn from their evil ways and to God.

But while the plagues were disastrous to the Egyptians, they were a sign of God's favor to the Jews. And it was through the divine intervention of God on behalf of the Jews that the angel of death would "Passover" the houses of God's people, on that dreadful night when the firstborn of every Egyptian family died.

So the natural catastrophes that were to be sent to the Earth could be seen as a judgment against the evil, but as a sign of God's favor to the righteous. And the trumpet that is meant to warn those who are in need of warning is the welcome sound of the voice of God to those who are listening for God to speak.

It would be difficult to imagine a scene of greater horror than the one pictured by the writer of Revelation in this chapter. The bottomless pit, belching black smoke so thick that it obliterated the sun, unrelenting torture and the despairing pleas for death to end misery, and an invasion of locusts that had the sting of a scorpion. What evil can possibly be referred to in such frightening symbols?

The horror mounts as the blurred vision of indescribable terror begins to be clarified a bit. What looked like locusts are really more like horses arrayed for battle. The riders have human faces, and crowns (or helmets, perhaps) on their heads. Iron breastplates protect them. And they are under the command of the exalted leader who presides from his place in the bottomless pit.

Isn't it possible that the Roman armies, which struck terror into the hearts of the entire world, were depicted here? And the exalted leader must surely be Domitian, the evil Caesar, whose renewed persecutions against the Christians were even more devastating than those ordered by Nero. And if there were a capital of evil in this world, a bottomless pit of desperate depravity, would it not be Rome?

And if the number of the hordes of Roman soldiers did not equal the number suggested here ("twice ten thousand times ten thousand" or two hundred million) their ranks must have looked as uncountable as they were unconquerable to those unfortunate enough to have been caught in the way of their advance.

In 1864, following the capture and burning of Atlanta, General William Tecumseh Sherman led his sixty thousand troops in a march all the way to the East coast, with the intent of destroying everything in their path. They burned houses and crops and killed farm animals and wrecked factories and railroads, in the attempt to deprive the Confederacy of anything that might be useful to the South's armies. Some of their opponents called Sherman's army "the wrath of God," seeing in their complete destruction the event foreshadowed in the horde of locusts depicted in Revelation.

But God is not angry, and enlists no earthly army to express divine displeasure. But such terrifying forces are at work in this world, and there is only one safe shelter from them: the hollow of God's hand.

Once again the writer of Revelation employs the suspense-stretching device of revealing the sixth in a series of seven items, then taking a delaying diversion before revealing the seventh. This time it is the seventh trumpet whose blast is postponed while we are invited to ponder the cryptic message of a scroll that is sweet to the mouth when eaten, but bitter in the stomach. Here is a message with three points, the first of which is this: If one is to represent God, it is essential for that person to take the whole message into his life, to assimilate it, to digest it, to make it a part of his or her entire being.

The Christian faith has no room for dilettantes who bring only a superficial curiosity to the great mysteries of the faith. Being a Christian may not take much of a man or woman, but it requires all that he or she is and has.

There is a vivid picture of this complete giving of self to the message of God in the last chapter of Genesis. After Joseph had welcomed his whole family into Egypt, where he could provide for them, Joseph required his brothers and their heirs to promise that when they returned to the homeland of Canaan, they would carry his bones back home. He was saying, in effect, I have given my life, I have given my past and present, I have given my strength. Now I want to give my bones, my future. To my faith in God I give all that I am or have or ever will be.

So the word of God must become a part of the messenger, as though he had actually eaten and digested it. And that word is sweet to the taste, as the psalmists had declared. It is sweet because it reminds us that our God is a communicating God, a God who reaches out to us and wishes to establish a relationship with us.

But that message, when eaten, is bitter in the stomach. There is a figure here that most twenty-first century people understand from their own experience. A sweet treat may very well cause indigestion that interrupts the sleep of the sufferer and may make him wish he had never indulged in the dessert.

So it is a delightful experience to be the recipient of a message from God. But the message may be painful to digest. What if God's message is a call to sacrificial discipleship? Once you have heard such a message, you cannot pretend you never received it. You are responsible for every word of God that you have heard.

As we have noted previously, the book of Revelation is one of a small collection of writings spoken of as "apocryphal." The word itself means "hidden" or "disguised." There were a few other writings incorporated into the biblical canon that share the same kind of arcane expression. Probably the greatest example, other than Revelation itself, is the Old Testament book of Daniel.

At the time Daniel was written, the Jews were suffering one of the most terrible times in their entire history. In 168 B.C. Antiochus Epiphanes and his armies invaded the weakened city of Jerusalem and took it captive. The invaders tried to stamp out the Hebrew faith in God, and to install in its place the Greek religion and culture. The temple was profaned. More than 80,000 Jews were slaughtered or sold into slavery. It was made a capital offense to observe any Jewish religious customs.

A gallant and heroic soldier named Judas Maccabaeus and his followers waged war against the Greek invaders, and pulled off a stunning victory, which is still celebrated today in the Jewish Feast of Hanukkah. But the period of time in which Jerusalem was held in the grip of such cruel and profane foreigners was from June 168 B.C. to December 165 B.C.–a period of three and a half years.

Daniel reported the period of three and a half years in his apocryphal writing as "a time, two times and a half a time" (a year, two years, and half a year, which would amount to 42 months, or three and a half years).

So the Seer of Patmos, in describing the time of woe and sorrow that would befall the Earth, said it would be forty-two months (or a time, two times, and half a time.) In this encrypted message, the writer is saying (in a symbolic language that the Christians would understand but the Romans would not) that the Christians faced an ordeal similar to that faced by the people of Jerusalem when Antiochus Epiphanes and his armies invaded.

Here was a word of warning, but also a word of hope. Forty-two months may seem like a long time, but it is not forever. "This too shall pass" runs a familiar saying. Or as the psalm said it, "Weeping may linger for the night, but joy comes with the morning" (Psalm 30:5).

DAY 161

A New Englander was shingling his house, but the fog was so dense that he could not see where the roof ended and the fog began, so, as he later reported it, "I shingled right off onto the fog." Such a mistake would be easy to make in trying to make sense of this particularly difficult chapter of Revelation. There are so many vivid details, and one is tempted to read some special significance into each one. And perhaps there is an intended significance, or it may be that the writer simply added all the details to heighten the sense of mystery and gravity. And it is clear that some images were formed by the Seer's knowledge of the Old Testament.

But like the parables of Jesus, this dramatic picture was intended by the writer to tell one truth, and it is surely this: Like the depicted woman, the church (or the community of the people of God) gave birth to a male child (Jesus) who was destined to rule all the Earth. Further, this community of God's chosen ones was (and is) subject to the determined persecution of the forces of evil. Finally, and in the face of all the persecutions and slanders, the community of God's people will survive and triumph, because God has pledged all the resources of heaven to protect and support it.

Note that the period of turmoil was predicted to last one thousand two hundred sixty days, which, once again, may be translated into forty-two months, or three and a half years, or Daniel's "time, two times, and half a time." So John was not foretelling a second period of distress, but reprising his earlier prediction of a time of persecution and suffering–a period through which the church (the community of God's people) was passing at that time.

There seemed to be no escape for the woman in John's picture (and no escape for the community of God's people from the persecutions of Rome), but then a way of escape is found: The woman is borne up on eagle's wings to a place of refuge in the desert. Eagles' wings are frequently seen, in biblical literature, as a reference to God's protective and empowering care. Remember Isaiah's word: "Those who wait for the LORD shall renew their strength; they shall mount up with wings like eagles" (Isaiah 40:31).

The imagery deepens, the mystery heightens, the meaning becomes clearer when we get to this chapter of Revelation. Remember that the Christians in Asia Minor (members of the seven congregations to which this book of Revelation was addressed) were daily faced with persecution specifically ordered by Domitian, the Roman emperor. To the Christians, therefore, there were two supreme enemies that threatened their very lives, and the life of their church: they were the Roman Empire and its supreme leader, the emperor Domitian.

Although Domitian was the current leader, for decades the Christians spoke of the emperor as Nero, because he was the Caesar who had initiated the bloodbath that plagued them. So it could be expected that when Domitian was spoken of in this writing, he would be called "Nero."

But there are two beasts that are described as desperately evil and powerful, and who derived their power and authority from Satan himself. The first beast clearly represents the Roman Empire—rising out of the sea, wearing the horns and crowns that prove its power and majesty, and bearing a resemblance to wild animals in its ferocity. But what is depicted as the second beast? The writer here gives a clue that his readers would find illuminating, but which the enemies would not understand. He said the beast had a "human number" of 666.

That number has for centuries inspired horror stories and fueled the imagination. Every generation has come up with its own candidate for the evil leader who would wear that number. One of the most ludicrous explanations is that the "evil beast" was the political leader whose three names were each spelled with six letters: Ronald Wilson Reagan.

But as noted previously, the ancient peoples had no specific characters to represent numerical values. Instead they assigned numerical values to letters of their alphabet. When spelled in its Latin (or Roman) letters, the numerical value of the numbers, added together, spell *Neron* (or Nero).

What word of value for us can be drawn from this teaching of such horrible evil?

Consider this: the world's greatest evil (which was how John depicted the Roman Empire and its leader) is nowhere to be found in this world. On the other hand, the Christians, who seemed only to be like cannon fodder in that great war between evil and good, are remembered as conquering saints. Whose side do you want to be on?

"And I heard a voice from heaven saying,…'Blessed *are* the dead who from now on die in the Lord'" (v. 13). Surely there is no more promising or encouraging word in the entire Bible than this assurance. The great good news is expressed in the first four words of that announcement from heaven's voice: "Blessed *are* the dead…"

What a chilling realization steals over us when a loved one has died, and we suddenly find it difficult and painful to speak of that person in only the past tense. Many a tear has been shed as we try to adjust to such a sudden cessation of time for our loved one, as though his watch had stopped, and the only existence left for him is in our memory.

But here comes this voice from heaven—God's own voice—saying, "Your loved one may still be spoken of in the present tense, and even in the future tense. He lives, and will yet live for eternities to come!" If you know any better news than that, then you have surely never stood beside the new grave of one you loved.

And not only do our loved ones continue to live, they continue to receive the blessing of the Almighty God. "Blessed are the dead who die in the Lord." Exactly what those divine blessings will consist of, we have no faculties to perceive. But surely there is no need that will not be graciously fulfilled, no hunger or thirst that is not abundantly satisfied, no capacity for joy that is not filled to the brim.

But the voice of God does not make this wholesale promise, but only to those "who die in the Lord." This was surely intended as encouragement to those who would shortly have to suffer martyrdom. Not only those who die in God's service, but also those who live in God's service will be counted among the redeemed in heaven.

It is believed that the apostle John, whom many believe to be the author of Revelation, was the only one of the original twelve who did not die as a martyr to his faith. He would surely have been willing to give that ultimate sacrifice, but it was never required of him. But he lived out his years in such faith and with such integrity that every day he lived was a benediction. And surely this "undying martyr" also found the crown of blessing given, as a perpetual reward, to those who die—or live—in the Lord.

DAY 164
Read Revelation 15

We are almost–but not quite–ready to leave behind the terrors and tribulations of the Earth and all its evil. First we must give our attention to a final set of seven images. Earlier in Revelation we saw the seven seals, and the seven trumpets. Now we are ready for the seven bowls containing the "wrath of God"–the judgment of God, in the form of seven plagues to chasten and refine the Earth.

As we have noted, the numbers seven and three were particularly meaningful in the vocabulary of all apocalyptic literature. Each was believed to be a holy number: seven represented the seven days of God's labor in creating the earth, and three pointed to the triune manifestations of God in the trinity. So three sets of seven would mean completion, the ultimate perfection.

Before the angels are dispatched to pour out the bowls of divine judgment upon the earth, we are given a glimpse of a worship service in heaven. In this glorious scene, the uncountable choir of martyrs and faithful believers sings a song of praise to God on the throne. The song of praise is, in itself, an amalgamation of various phrases from the psalms. But what is noteworthy about it is that not one word is said or sung by the choir of the faithful about their own victory, their own faithfulness, or their own labors–as praiseworthy as they might have been. Their attention was fixed entirely upon God.

Perhaps that says something about the attitude that got them to heaven in the first place: They were not always thinking of themselves, not always scheming to gain some advantage over others, not always interpreting events in terms of how they would affect their own personal lives. They were focused outward and upward.

The lyrical gospel of Luke closes with the note that the followers of Christ "were continually in the temple blessing God" (Luke 24:53). What? With a church to establish, a kingdom to bring in, a world to save, they were spending time in the temple praising God? Yes, and that may explain where their power and vision came from. Even when we get to heaven, there will be ample reason to praise God. For "the LORD is worthy to be praised" (2 Samuel 22:4).

After once again teasing us with a suspense-stretching interlude, the Seer of Patmos is now ready to show us the final devastation on the Earth, when the seven angels pour out their bowls of divine wrath. And the catastrophes that follow sound a great deal like the ten plagues visited upon Pharaoh and his Egypt, when Moses came to deliver the people of Israel from their bondage. In fact, several of the plagues on Egypt are identical to the calamities visited upon the Earth when the angels poured out their bowls of divine wrath. There was water turning to blood, the thunder, the hail, and the pervasive darkness.

John's readers would remember the story of Moses and the plagues and would surely draw the parallel that we must: that such visitations, whatever their source, are times of testing and judgment. Beyond that recognition, however, there is a theological problem: Is it God who sends calamities upon us?

It is quite common after a natural disaster such as a tornado, earthquake, or flood, for people to ask, "Why did God do this to us?" Or at least, "Why did God let this happen?" One can easily identify with their suffering, and it may not be appropriate at such a time to engage a fellow sufferer in a theological debate. But we must surely defend the honor of God. Unlike the Hebrew people, who believed that every natural event had been personally instigated by God, we know that in this universe there is such a thing as an accident, and that there are those with evil intent who exercise the freedom of will God gave all human beings, to effect great sorrow and suffering. When God is blamed for widespread disease, pain, suffering, and deprivation, I want to ask, "With a Friend like that, who needs enemies?"

But God does utilize every tool that fits his hand, to teach us lessons we need to learn and arrive at conclusions that we need to draw. And if the people of the Earth need to be brought to their knees in humility, the Earth itself has in its repertoire of misfortune, all kinds of untoward events, that can accomplish that. But when that happens, God will be there to help the sufferer find healing and the strength to start anew.

It would be difficult to overstate the antipathy the Christians—Jewish and Gentile alike—had toward the Roman Empire. The Romans destroyed the city of Jerusalem and its temple, which was the pride of every Jew. The Christians were chased out of Jerusalem and hounded from country to country by the Roman conquerors. While the Romans barely tolerated Christianity in its earlier years, the empire's patience had reached the breaking point by the end of the first century. Partly to goad the Christians into acts of disobedience that would result in their execution, the Roman Caesars began to require that all their citizens worship them as gods. In the reign of Domitian (who was often thought to be Nero returned from the dead) this emperor worship had reached the point of being an absolute demand, on pain of death. The Christians had given up their homelands, their freedom, their families, and in some cases, their very lives, in order not to give up the one thing that meant the most to them: their faith.

It was, therefore, a combination of religious fervor and ethnic pride that made John's demonizing pictures of Rome and its Caesars so appealing. Without doubt, when in secret assemblies the churches read aloud this broadside, there must have been cheering and the singing of praises when the Seer's vivid pictures foretold the defeat of Rome and the one who sat on its throne.

So once again John depicts Rome in a most unflattering figure: a prostitute, dressed in purple (to signify royalty and riches) and scarlet (to represent the sinful ways of the woman). But despite the apparent security of this wicked woman, the time will come, John prophecies, when she will be utterly defeated and destroyed. And the countries and armies that accomplish the defeat of this wicked woman (or the city of Rome) would be seen as accomplishing the will of God.

Few people can have the far-reaching power or wealth of this fictitious woman. But assuming, for a moment, that we could possess those treasures, could they buy one moment of peace and joy if we realized that *someone in Heaven wants us dead?*

Here we have a literary form known as a "Doom Song." Examples of this kind of song, celebrating the downfall of evil, may be found in several books of the Old Testament. Although the fall of Rome would not happen for several more centuries, so certain was John that it would take place that he reports it in the past tense, as though Rome's demise has already taken place.

Of special interest in this "Doom Song" is the precaution taken on behalf of those who might be living in the doomed city, but who were the people of God. A voice from heaven warns them: "Come out of her, my people." It was a call to God's people to separate themselves from associations that were alien to their faith and would, therefore, lead them to share the destruction of their environment.

God's challenge has always been a call to "come out." God summoned Abraham to "come out" of his home in Ur of the Chaldees, to go to a place that God would show him. Through Moses God called the people of Israel out of their Egyptian bondage and to a land of promise. And when Jesus established his church, it bore the name of *ekklesia,* which is Greek for "the called-out ones."

Speaking through Paul's second letter to the Corinthians, Paul said, "Come out from them, and be separate from them, says the Lord" (2 Corinthians 6:17). We must be reminded that espousing the Christian faith almost invariably meant painful separations for the early Christians. Frequently their stand isolated them from family, from friends, from work, and from social life.

When the Risen Christ appeared to the fishermen-disciples after the resurrection, Jesus asked Peter three times (perhaps to allow Peter to retract his three denials of Christ on the evening of his betrayal), "Do you love me?" One of those questions went a bit further: "Do you love me more than these?" Was Jesus referring to the fish, or the other apostles, or some other entities? We don't know. But it's just as well that the question is left open-ended. Do you love him more than ——? You finish that statement, by inserting whatever people or things or pleasures contend with your loyalty to Christ. Whatever that association is, Christ's challenge to you is: "Come out!"

Finally, after a long description of Earth's various evils and the portents, omens, and symbols that point to them, we come to the victory celebration. The war is over! The new day has broken! Right is seated permanently on the throne, and wrong has been buried in a locked grave. There is much to celebrate, or would be, when John's prophecies—phrased confidently in the past tense of the fait accompli—are all fulfilled.

So the heavenly choirs sang their Hallelujahs, the martyrs and angels joining their voices with all the other denizens of heaven. And John, receiving a personal message from God, delivered to him personally by an angel, fell down to worship the angelic messenger. But the angel corrected this breach of heavenly protocol: "You must not do that! I am a fellow servant with you and your brethren who hold the testimony of Jesus."

It was an important distinction, and one that John needed to relay to the Christian congregations that would read his words. In that culture, dominated by polytheism, there was a tendency on the part of the Christians to find other objects for their veneration. Yes, to be sure, God was the one and only deity, but couldn't they spare a little veneration for angels, who were perpetually in God's presence, and whose faces shone from that divine communion? Even John had invited the churches to remember that each congregation had a guardian and guiding angel. What would be wrong with worshiping the angels?

But anything or anyone that is worshiped instead of God is an idol, and idolatry is always a sin.

The tendency in these days is to find other objects to worship. Some churches are bibliolatrous—they worship the Bible. And the Bible contains God's word, but it is only a tool, and does not deserve our reverence. Some churches worship their own rituals or worship patterns, but, again, these are only instruments by which we worship God, and the instrument must never receive the adoration meant for God alone. Some churches adore their own set of criteria, by which they decide who is worthy to be called a child of God. But God is not pleased with such efforts to take out of his hand the prerogative of deciding who gets to have communion with the divine.

It is God, only God, who is holy and wholly deserving of our praise. Worshiping anything else is blasphemy.

For centuries the battle has been waged, and no armistice is in sight. It is not a battle between good and evil, nor even a battle between Christ and the antichrist, but rather a theological skirmish between the premillennialists and the postmillennialists. The former believe that the second coming of Christ will introduce that thousand years of peace, as opposed to the latter, who believe that Christ's return will follow that thousand-year period. Such mole-eyed literalists have let the grand truth of Revelation be frittered away in frivolous squabbles over symbols that were never meant to be taken as verbatim descriptions of actual events.

When one considers the energy expended in such fruitless speculations through the years, one feels the need to ask, "What's the difference?" All the while breath and printer's ink have been invested in this controversy, babies have been born, wars have been waged, nations have risen and fallen, and it is likely that not one person has been brought closer to God or become more devoted to addressing human need because of these arcane doctrines.

Can we not just accept the fact that written into the destiny of this world is the remembrance that God is in charge and that God has already determined that, just as there was a beginning of this world, there will be an ending? And the same God who was present "in the beginning" will be present "in the end." And that end will not be because God has given up on the world—which would make God a loser—but the end will come when Earth has served the purpose for which God created it.

And it will be a time of rejoicing, and a time of peace at last. And perhaps the people of God will, by that time, have discovered how futile is war and the human hatred that fuels it, and will discover and experience—for a thousand years or so—the shalom that God meant for the Earth's climate.

And our job, in the meantime, is not to speculate about future events (remembering that Jesus warned us, "It is not for you to know the times or periods that the Father has set by his own authority" [Acts 1:7]), but to add our prayers and efforts to those of our God, who still hopes that day of eternal peace will come soon.

DAY 170
Read Revelation 21

What a magnificent depiction of heaven is presented to us when we read this chapter of Revelation. Since the glories of heaven cannot be perceived by our limited faculties, we must depend upon similes and metaphors to tell us what we cannot see or understand, but what our hearts hunger to claim. And even previously employed figures of speech by which John described what he had seen in heaven are now left behind. No more golden streets or gates of pearl or emerald and ruby fountains. But one meaningful symbol tells us all we need to know: "a bride adorned for her husband." Anyone who has been a bride, or has been the mother or father of the bride, will surely remember the meticulous care given to every detail of the bride's appearance. A costly new dress, just the right jewels, shoes to match the dress, the grooming and makeup subjected to the most careful scrutiny. And John says that's how heaven looks.

But, ah, the real beauty of heaven is not what the eye can see or the mind can conceive, but what the heart cherishes: It is the companionship that makes heaven heaven. And that companionship is blessed indeed. Not only are loved ones present in heaven, to greet us when we arrive, and not only those who have inspired us to live lives that aimed us toward heaven, but there is another whose eternal companionship will make our joy complete. That one is God. "The home of God is among mortals," John says, in astonished ecstasy. "He will dwell with them; they will be his peoples, and God himself will be with them." (So amazed is John by this fact that he repeats it!) "He will wipe every tear from their eyes. Death will be no more; mourning and crying and pain will be no more, for the first things have passed away" (vv. 3, 4).

"Every generous act of giving, with every perfect gift, is from above, coming down from the Father of lights," James said (James 1:17). And that one who has at his fingertips every resource, and who knows what you need before you need it, loves you quite as though you were the only child God had. And that one has promised to be with you forever.

What more could anyone ask?

In the beginning, according to the book of Genesis, there was a beautiful place, where, among all the varieties of vegetation, there were two trees. One was the tree of life, whose fruit, when consumed, would confer eternal life. The other was the tree of the knowledge of good and evil. Contrary to the assumption of many casual readers, it was not the tree of life whose fruit Adam and Eve ate, but rather the tree of the knowledge of good and evil. And for that disobedience, the first human pair was expelled from the garden. Thus begins the story of the human race. It begins with rebellion, with a wrong choice, and with the far-reaching consequences of that disobedience.

Why didn't Adam and Eve eat of the tree of life? Apparently there was no injunction put upon them to keep them from enjoying the fruit of that tree. And what a delight they would have experienced in eating that fruit, for it was the food of eternal life.

When Adam and Eve were expelled, God stationed a cherubim with a flaming sword to guard the tree of life. In all the ensuing centuries, the people of God longed to be given the right to eat of that tree, and thereby claim immortality. Perhaps it was to answer this longing that Peter said of Jesus, "His own self bare our sins in his own body on the tree, that we, being dead to sins, should live unto righteousness" (1Peter 2:24, KJV). Could that be the "tree of life"?

Except for a symbolic reference in the book of Ezekiel (Ezekiel 47:12) we do not hear again about the tree of life until the book of Revelation, in which the Spirit of Christ says to the congregation at Ephesus, "To everyone who conquers, I will give permission to eat from the tree of life that is in the paradise of God" (Revelation 2:7). Then, finally, in the last chapter of Revelation the tree is shown as fully accessible. It has different fruits every month, and its leaves are for the healing of the nations. That tree yields whatever "fruit" is needed to meet any need bountifully, and all people, of every nation, may find healing in it.

So the whole story of the Bible, indeed the entire saga of human life, is really the account of a tree being lost, then found again. And in the restoration of that tree to the center of the lives of God's children, there is depicted the second chance the Creator gives the human family.

It is also the story of two trees, one that represents disobedience to God and that yields sorrow, and the other tree, which represents compliance with the holy will and which yields joy. Which do you choose?